Be

CW01640691

THE DIVISIONS INVOLVED IN THE NORMANDY LANDINGS

To my brother Laurent, who passed his passion for the Normandy Landings on to me, and who was the first to introduce me to this great battle.

Editions OUEST-FRANCE

The battle of Normandy involved six land armies from the two camps: two American *(1st* and *3rd US Armies)*, two British *(2nd British Army, 1st Canadian Army)* and two German (*VII. Army* and *V. Panzer Army*, originally known as *Panzergruppe West*). These armies were subdivided into army corps, with multiple divisions as well as independent units. The division (10,000 to 20,000 men) is in effect the lynchpin of any army. It is, in fact, a scaled-down army in itself, able to carry out all sorts of tasks autonomously. The officer in charge of a division, most often a general, is the one who, on the tactical plan, will implement the decisions taken by the High Command.

The division is normally commanded by a general. Each regiment (2,000 to 3,000 men, commanded by a colonel) is divided into battalions (800 to 1,000 men with a battalion commander), which are themselves divided into companies (180 men with a captain) comprising several sections (35 to 40 men with a lieutenant), which are organized into combat groups (10 to 12 men with a sergeant). With a few differences, all armies and all types of divisions (infantry, armoured, parachute, etc.) conform to a similar plan.

An infantry division usually aligns three infantry regiments (two within some German units) and one artillery regiment (or several battalions), as well as various support units: anti-tank battalion, DCA (communications) battalion, reconnaissance battalion, engineer battalion, transport battalion, medical unit. Far from being composed only of tanks, an armoured division is organized in a similar manner: one or two tank regiments side by side with one or two infantry regiments. Sometimes, certain independent units are temporarily attached to the division; in this way, a number of American divisions were attached to a tank battalion and a battalion of *Tank Destroyers*, which consisted of a hundred armoured vehicles. These non-divisional independent units also exist at army level.

The Anglo-Canadian infantry is an exception, since a brigade is equivalent to a regiment in the other

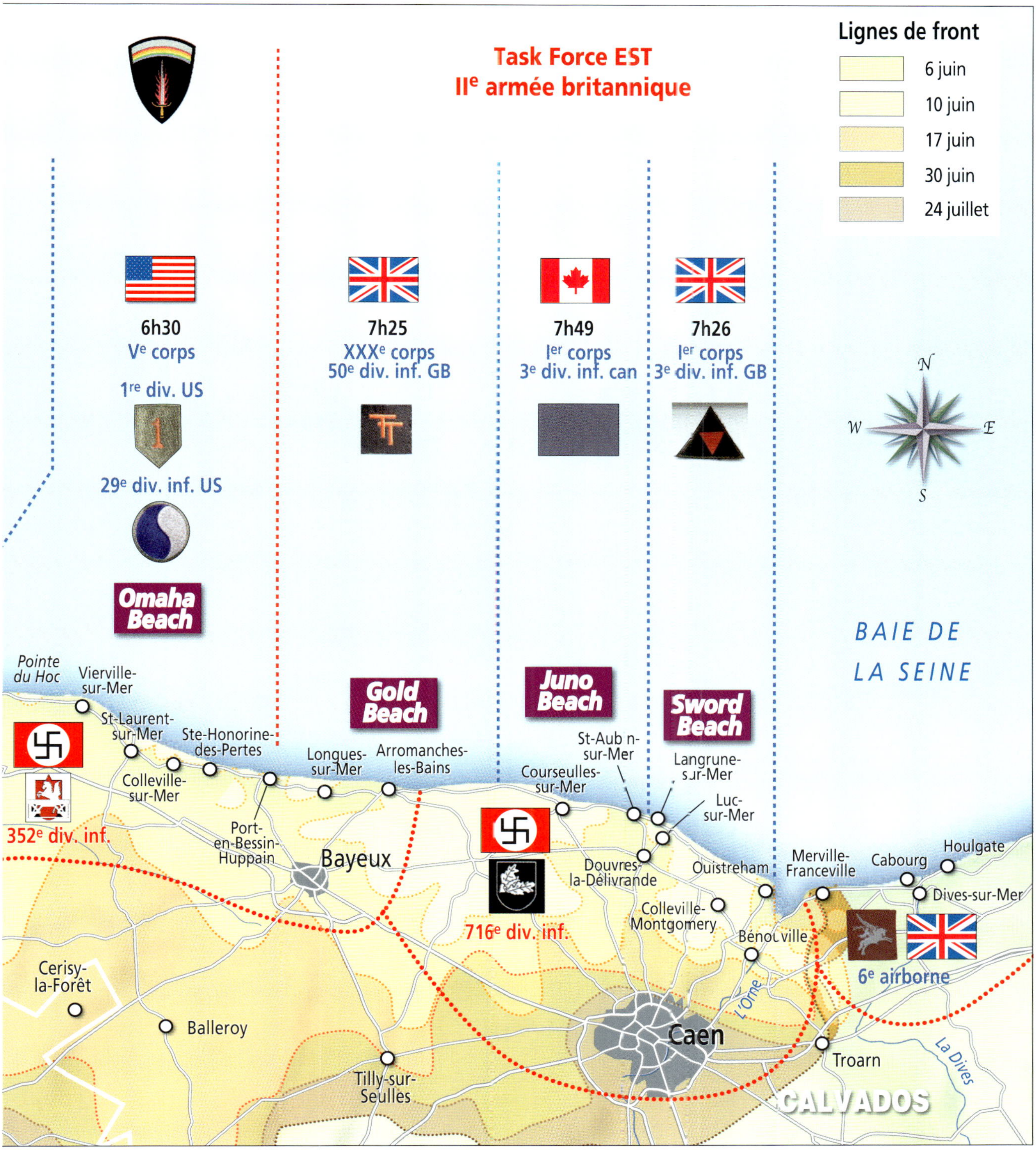

Task Force EST
IIe armée britannique
Lignes de front
6 juin
10 juin
17 juin
30 juin
24 juillet
6h30
Ve corps
1re div. US
29e div. inf. US
Omaha Beach
7h25
XXXe corps
50e div. inf. GB
Gold Beach
7h49
Ier corps
3e div. inf. can
Juno Beach
7h26
Ier corps
3e div. inf. GB
Sword Beach
N
W
E
S
BAIE DE LA SEINE
Pointe du Hoc
Vierville-sur-Mer
St-Laurent-sur-Mer
Colleville-sur-Mer
Ste-Honorine-des-Pertes
Port-en-Bessin-Huppain
Longues-sur-Mer
Arromanches-les-Bains
Bayeux
352e div. inf.
Courseulles-sur-Mer
St-Aubin-sur-Mer
Langrune-sur-Mer
Luc-sur-Mer
Douvres-la-Délivrande
716e div. inf.
Colleville-Montgomery
Ouistreham
Bénouville
Merville-Franceville
Cabourg
Houlgate
Dives-sur-Mer
6e airborne
L'Orne
Caen
Troarn
La Dives
Cerisy-la-Forêt
Balleroy
Tilly-sur-Seulles
CALVADOS

CHAIN OF COMMAND OF THE ALLIED ARMY AT AUGUST 1, 1944

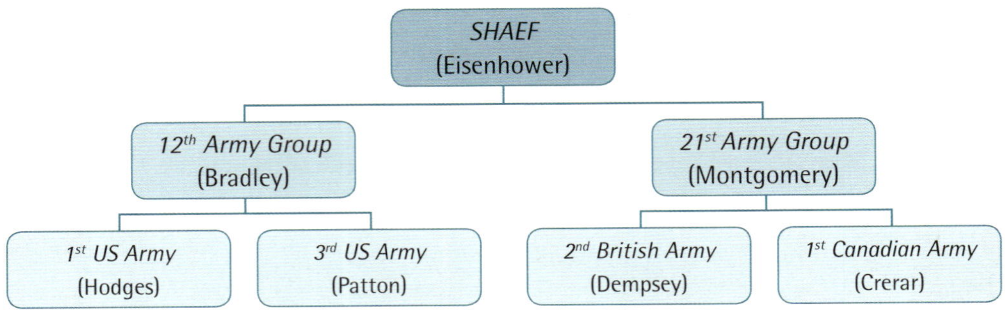

CHAIN OF COMMAND OF THE GERMAN ARMY ON THE EVENING OF JUNE 6, 1944

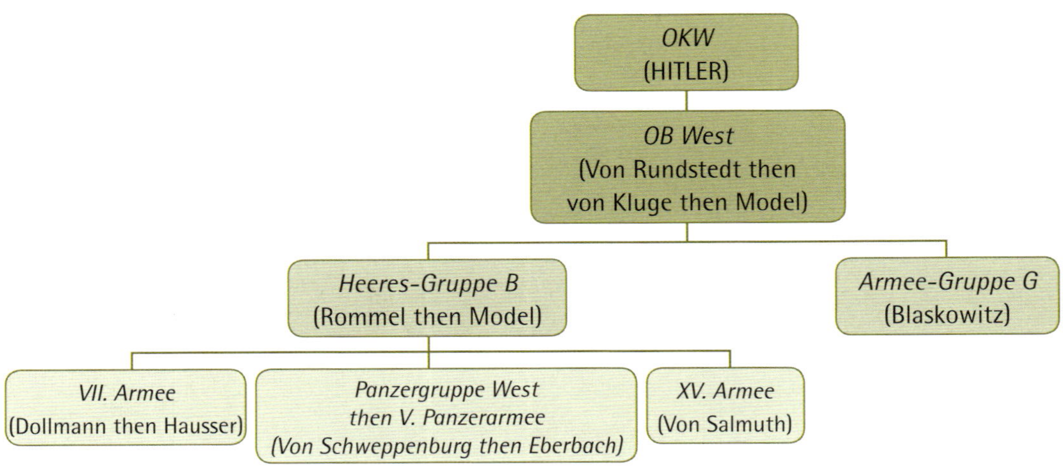

armies. What the British army call a regiment is in fact an administrative unit. Each regiment provides as many battalions as the number of recruits from the county permits. These battalions are then dispersed among different divisions. In this way, *1st Suffolk Regiment* was the first battalion of the regiment raised in Suffolk. Similarly, the Regina Rifle *Regiment* was in fact a battalion.

The feats of weapons and the campaigns led by some of these divisions have made them the most famous and prestigious units of the conflict. More than armies and regiments, and even more than the army corps, the collective memory retains the divisions above all. Some of the smaller units - for example, the *Fallschirmjäger-Regiment 6* or even the *Rangers* - or of a different nature, such as the *III*

The entire general staff of SHAEF (Supreme Headquarters Allied Expeditionary Forces). Left to right: Lieutenant-General Omar Bradley, Admiral Bertram Ramsay, Air Chief Marshall Sir Arthur Tedder, General Dwight D. Eisenhower, General Sir Bernard Montgomery, Air Chief Marshall Sir Trafford Leigh-Mallory, Lieutenant-General Walter Bedell Smith. NARA

Flak-Korps, however, followed an autonomous course, crucial to the course of the battle, which justifies their presentation within this book.

In spite of the vast number of works on the battle of Normandy, there was no history of the landing from the point of view of the divisions. Fifty-one units or types of units have been selected as representative of the 83 divisions and dozens of independent units who took part in the battle of Normandy. The path of each division in Normandy is described here, with a particularly significant battle fought by each unit highlighted.

6th British Airborne Division

A British paratroop harnessed in the straps of his parachute, as he would have appeared on June 6, with his 'legpack' allowing him to carry additional equipment. Across his chest, the man is wearing a cartridge belt for a Sten gun magazine, typical of airborne troops. Unusually, it has been daubed with camouflage paint. Coll. T. Le Sant

The decision to establish Major-General Gale's division was taken on April 23, 1943. D-Day was his first engagement. Fully trained, duly selected and ready for battle with the enemy, the British paratroopers - who had adopted the nickname of *Red Devils*, given to them by their adversaries in Tunisia - were aware that they constituted an elite unit with a strong spirit of camaraderie. The *6th Airborne*, 12,500 men strong, included two *Parachute Brigades* (the *3rd* and *5th*) and the *6th Airlanding Brigade*. The usual support troops complemented the organisation of the division, including one hundred anti-tank vehicles, twenty-seven howitzers and a reconnaissance regiment of which the armoured section included eleven light *Tetrarch* tanks. The airborne division lacked heavy weapons, and its mobility was considerably reduced, but these drawbacks were not important because liaison with the troops taking part in amphibious landings had to be carried out quickly.

A Corporal of the 6th Airborne. The Red Devils' silhouette was very different from the normal Tommy's: they wore the airborne forces steel helmet and a camouflage uniform. The toggle rope they carried round their shoulders was very useful for men who had fallen into marshes, or were hanging from trees. Coll. T. Le Sant

A perfect landing! An ingenious system allowed the back of the Horsa to be detached from the rest of the fuselage, so allowing the machinery or ordnance aboard to be unloaded. NARA

With its silent approach, carrying 28 soldiers, the Horsa glider was ideal to carry out a *coup de main*. Royal Air Force

The *6th Airborne* was entrusted with a task of the utmost importance in the context of *Operation Overlord*. This was to secure the left flank of the entire operation. To do so, Gale had to seize the bridges over the Orne at Ranville and its canal at Bénouville, and destroy those which crossed the Dives and the Divette at Bures, Robehomme and Troarn. But first, they had to establish

Pegasus, the winged horse, ridden by Bellerophon: a suitable emblem for the Parachute Regiment. This was the idea of Daphne du Maurier, wife of 'Boy' Browning, known as the father of the British airborne troops Coll. T. Le Sant

PEGASUS BRIDGE

The work of Major Howard's men on the bridge of Bénouville on the night of June 5 - 6 has passed into history. This feat of arms was the result of an operation meticulously prepared in England. They made a reduced-scale model of the bridge and its defences, regularly updated, and training was carried out on a similar site near Exeter. *Operation Deadstick* foresaw that a company, strengthened by the *Oxfordshire and Buckinghamshire Light Infantry,* aboard six Horsa gliders - the 'silent coffins', as those being carried called them - could seize intact the bridges on the Orne river and its canal, at Ranville and Bénouville. Howard then had to ensure the defence until it was reinforced by the *7th Parachute Battalion,* nearly three hours later. Released shortly before reaching the French coast, the first *Horsa* arrived silently near its goal at 0:16, on June 6, 1944. In just a few minutes, *Pegasus Bridge* was secured. Shortly afterwards, Howard learned that the bridge at Ranville was also in the hands of his men. His radio operator, Corporal Tappenden, could then transmit the code *Ham and Jam* signifying the success of the operation.

Major Howard, the man who led the legendary assault on the bridge at Bénouville.

and consolidate a solid bridgehead to the east of the Orne, to thwart any attempt of the Germans to counter-attack in the direction of *Sword Beach*. The *6th Airborne* also secured the proper procedure of the landing operation, by moving on to neutralise the battery at Merville.

The *6th Airborne* performed all the tasks which were entrusted to it on D-Day, and the bridgehead was secured. On the evening of June 6, 7,200 men had been landed in Normandy, using 348 gliders. This success cost the loss of 1,022 men: 61 killed, 349 wounded and 612 missing. Strengthened by several units of the *1st British Corps*, the *Red Devils* waged a war of position up until August 16, a miscast role for such seasoned veterans. By mid-July, the *6th Airborne* had suffered the loss of 2,500 men, with only a reinforcement of 600 volunteers having counteracted the losses to a certain degree. The testing combat in the Bavent woods was followed by the relentless Allied advance up to the Seine, in the context of *Operation Paddle*. A number of villages in the Auge and on the Fleurie coast were liberated in

These four paratroops were the pathfinders of the 22nd Independent Parachute Company. They had to lay out the beacons on the drop and landing zones. The system of fastening the chin straps of the paratroops' helmets can be seen clearly here. NARA

Beyond Colombelles, Pegasus Bridge was the only crossing point downstream of Caen on the Orne canal. It had to be seized to protect the right flank of the landing zone. IWM

The hunting horn for their berets and the shoulder badge of the Oxfordshire & Buckinghamshire Regimen, of which Major John Howard's D Company of the 2nd Battalion formed the backbone of the soldiers in the Coup de Main party which seized Pegasus Bridge. Coll. T. Le Sant

this way by the British airborne troops. On August 26, they were at Pont Audemer. Retired from the front, the *6th Airborne* could count the cost. The losses amounted to 4,457 men: 821 killed, 2,709 wounded and 927 missing (including 878 prisoners).

The *6th Airborne* fought in the Ardennes and then, on March 24, 1945, took part in *Operation Varsity*, the crossing of the Rhine. They finished the war on the Baltic, where they made contact with the Red Army.

Two paras armed with Sten Mk Vs with wooden stocks, typical for the airborne troops. The 6th Airborne succeeded in seizing its objectives. They had to hold their positions. NARA

82nd US Airborne Division « All Americans »

In the face of the German airborne forces success in 1940, Major-General Ridgway's *82nd Airborne* was the first airborne division formed in the United States, at Fort Benning. The unit was engaged in 1942 in North Africa, and in 1943 in Sicily and then in Italy. The experience gained during these first battles was essential to the preparation of *Operation Overlord.* In June 1944, the division comprised approximately 9,000 men: it was given the mission of seizing bridges on the Merderet and in various communities, in particular the town of Sainte-Mère-Église. Its essential task was to protect the western flank of *Utah Beach* and to secure a solid bridgehead to the west of the Merderet, with the view of cutting off the Cotentin peninsula. The position of the *82nd Airborne* being considered particularly exposed, it was planned to strengthen it with Colonel Raff's *Task Force*, bringing together various units of the division and 21 *Sherman*, who had to charge on Sainte-Mère-Église as soon as they had landed on *Utah Beach* in the early afternoon.

This medic of the 82nd US Airborne has put on his jumping kit. The paras M2 helmet could be identified by its chinstrap. The model 42 jump jacket, although flattering and well equipped with cargo pockets, remained very fragile. To ensure his mission, this soldier carries medical equipment stowed in bags with reinforced straps. Coll. T. Le Sant

The fabric insignia of the 82nd US Airborne 'All Americans', worn on the left sleeve of the uniforms of the soldiers in that unit. Coll. T. Le Sant

Soldiers of the 325th Glider Infantry Regiment near their Horsa gliders. Looked down on by their parachuting comrades, these soldiers, who had not volunteered to serve in the airborne forces, still risked just as much as they did. NARA

On D-Day, the scouts were not able to fulfil their role properly, and the parachute drops were very much dispersed, due to the nervousness of many of the pilots, who were often novices. 6,400 men, transported in 377 aircraft and 52 gliders, were involved in missions *Boston* and *Chicago*, the dropping points of the *82nd*. The landing of the airborne fleet was not without difficulty, as many gliders crashed into the trees in hedges when setting down. There were 157 casualties, including 25 killed, among the 957 men who arrived by glider. If few men were operational, due to the scattered dropping zones, the confusion was worse among Germans, in the face of the multiple areas of parachute landings. Colonel Krause, commander of a battalion of the *505th*, secured Sainte-Mère-Église while various mixed forces attempted to secure the bridges of the Fière and the Chef-du-Pont. The control of these bridges was not won without bitter fighting, faced with a tenacious and determined enemy. In the evening, airborne reinforcements supported the *82nd*, but again, crashes were numerous (200 losses).

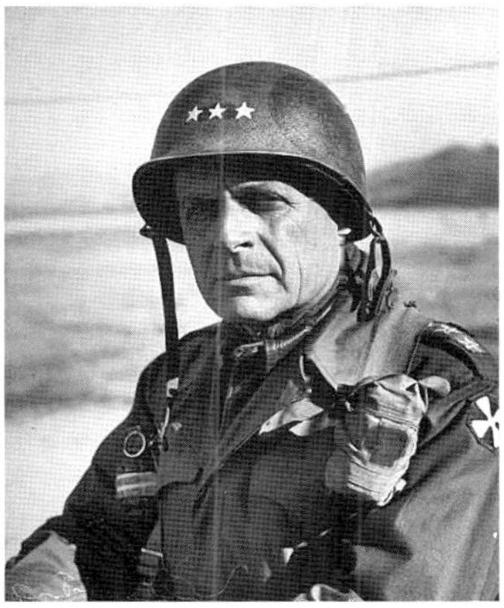

Matthew Ridgway, Commander of the 82nd US Airborne. His men were first of all inclined to see him as a 'leg', that is to say a non-paratrooper. However, he jumped with them on the night of June 6 ...

Lieutenant Kelso Horne, whose face reflects the exhaustion caused by several days of fierce fighting in the *bocage*. His 48-star flag can be clearly seen, as worn by the men of the 82nd US Airborne. NARA

The battle of Normandy was not finished for these men, who were plunged into the hell of the *bocage* for weeks. The *82nd Airborne* participated actively in the operations leading to the isolation of Cherbourg, by cutting off the Cotentin Peninsula after taking control of Saint-Sauveur-le-Vicomte. On July 3, the *82nd Airborne Division* was again on the offensive in the La Haye-du-Puits and Mont Castre sector. This costly operation represented the unit's last participation in the Battle of Normandy. On July 8, the division was finally relieved. On July 1, the division's losses were 5,429 men out of the 11,770 soldiers engaged in the conflict.

SAINTE-MÈRE-ÉGLISE

During the night, several sticks of the *82nd Airborne* landed on Sainte-Mère-Église, in an episode immortalised by Hollywood in *The Longest Day*. Some were killed, while two others remained suspended from the church by their parachutes. Ordered to take over the village, Lieutenant-Colonel Krause assembled one hundred and eighty men of his battalion after the parachute drop, making it one of the most successful drops on that fateful night. The objective, poorly defended, fell rapidly into his hands. Ten Germans were killed and thirty others were captured. Reinforced by Lieutenant-Colonel Vandervoort's battalion, they were confronted with a serious German counter-attack, supported by tanks, from the south around 09:30, while a small combat group stopped the Germans in the north, at Neuville. Sainte-Mère-Église was not retaken.

Sainte-Mère-Église: an important road junction which was one of the D-Day objectives of the 82nd US Airborne. 'The Longest Day' has immortalized the incredible story of John Steele, whose parachute remains attached to the church tower. Photo Isabelle Bournier

Restored to strength with the arrival and integration of reinforcements, the *82nd* participated in *Operation Market Garden* in September 1944, securing - not without difficulties - the taking of the bridge at Nijmegen. Its role during the Battle of the Bulge was particularly crucial in holding back the breakthrough of the *Panzers*. After having fought in the Ruhr, they finished the war on the Elbe.

The 'All Americans' of the 505th PIR of the 82nd. escort their prisoners in the Sainte-Mère-Église sector. They had succeeded in holding their position in the face of an enemy which was attacking in strength, but in a way which was not well enough coordinated to mobilise all its resources. Fierce fighting still awaited these GIs, until the end of July. NARA

This famous photograph was taken on June 8 in Saint-Marcouf. These paras, probably from the 502nd PIR, had retaken the village with the 4th US ID. Advancing still demanded prudence. The leading GI is taking the customary precautions: keeping a sharp lookout to the rear while the rest of the group moves forward along the street. NARA

Gliders allowed the delivery of essential heavy equipment, such as jeeps, of which 283 were in use within one US Airborne Division; but only a few dozen vehicles arrived by glider. Coll. T. Le Sant

101st US Airborne Division « Screaming Eagles »

On August 15 1942, some five months after the *82nd Airborne*, a second airborne division was set up: the *101st Airborne*, commanded by Major-General Taylor. Perfectly trained and with morale running high, the airborne forces' recruits were highly motivated. During

Like all his peers, this para of the 101st Airborne US wore a distinguishing badge on his helmet (Ace of Spades, of Hearts, etc.). His USM1 A1 rifle with its folding metal butt was the specific weapon for the airborne troops. The first-aid kit saved many lives. On the other hand, the anti-gas armband worn on the right shoulder was fortunately of no use. Coll. T. Le Sant

A para of the 101st, such as he would be upon boarding a C-47. The Mae West lifejacket was a necessity for a flight over the English Channel. Many paras also fell in flooded areas. This GI is wearing a reserve chest parachute as well as a 'legbag'. The dagger, duly strapped to the ankle, was used to free them from the harness.
Coll. T. Le Sant

exercises, the emphasis was very much on physical fitness, hand-to-hand combat and the handling of various weapons. The first combat test for the *Screaming Eagles* was no less than *Operation Overlord*, since the unit had not yet been under fire. The division was organized in a manner similar to the *82nd Airborne*, and comprised almost 9,000 men, three hundred jeeps, a hundred trucks, a hundred mortars, thirty-six 75mm howitzers and anti-tank guns.

The plan, decided in February 1944 and then amended, provided that the *101st* should support the landing at *Utah Beach* by securing various beach exits, neutralising several enemy strongholds and by securing the area north of Carentan to guard the bridgehead from any German counter-attack from this zone. The mission was therefore of the utmost importance. Concerned about the losses which had been predicted for the airborne forces, Eisenhower decided to meet men of the *502nd Parachute Infantry Regiment* shortly before their takeoff for Normandy.

The sleeve badge of the 101st US Airborne 'Screaming Eagles'. Coll. T. Le Sant

Lacking vehicles, these paras of the 101st use a Kübelwagen taken in Carentan. The little town, which commands the passage on the Vire, constituted an essential objective: contact had to be established between Utah Beach and Omaha Beach. NARA

If the Channel crossing was carried out without significant problems, the lack of experience of the transport aircraft pilots and the confusion caused by clouds and the firing of flak caused a wide dispersal of drop zones. The drop mission of the *101st* bore the code name *Albany*. The 6,900 men of

The men aboard the C-47s, faces blackened. The tension mounts, but the long wait is now over: it's time to fight at last! NARA

Eisenhower, very worried because of the losses which had been predicted, visited the paras of the 502nd PIR on the evening of June 5. Ike was reassured: the paras had good morale! NARA

Maxwell Taylor, Commander of the 101st US Airborne. Against all expectations, this officer of the 82nd US Airborne was designated to command the 101st after the removal of General Bill Lee, the father of the American airborne troops, for health reasons.
Caen Memorial

the three regiments transported by 485 aircraft and the airborne troops aboard 52 gliders suffered losses on landing because of the hedges, 'Rommel's asparagus' and the flooding in the Merderet marshes, in which many drowned, burdened by their heavy loads. However, the confusion among the enemy was even greater. By evening, they had joined forces with units of the *4th US Infantry Division* who had landed on *Utah Beach*. They managed to secure the exits from the beach. Further south, the *501st PIR* took control of the lock at La Barquette, on the Douve, but failed at Saint-Côme-du-Mont, defended by the *Fallschirmjäger* - their German counterparts. In the evening, the *Keokuk* mission allowed reinforcements to be brought in by glider (44 losses).

The *101st Airborne Division* then proceeded to take Carentan on June 12, not without previously having surprised and wiped out an entire battalion of Major von der Heydte's *Fallschirmjäger*. The attempt to regain the town by the *SS* of the *17.SS Panzer-Grenadier -Division* was repelled by the *Screaming Eagles*. At the beginning of July, after three weeks at the front, the division was retired, to be repatriated to England. As of July 1, its total losses amounted to 4,670 men, including many who were missing.

Less than a month after the conclusion of the battle of Normandy, the *101st Airborne* was involved in the airborne *Operation Market Garden*, launched over Holland. The division's moment of glory was the epic defence of Bastogne, in the course of the Battle of the Bulge. At the end of the war, part of the unit went as far as the *Führer's* mountain retreat, at Berchtesgaden.

THE SECURING OF THE BEACH EXITS

At the north of the dropping zones, Colonel Van Horn Moseley Jr's *502nd,* landing on *Drop Zone A,* established defence positions at Foucarville and Beuzeville-au-Plain while securing the control of *Exit 4* (exit no. 4 from *Utah Beach*), without having had to take the Saint-Martin-de-Varreville battery, already neutralized by bombing. Lieutenant-Colonel Cole's *3/502* secured control of *Exit 3*. South of the *Utah Beach* area, *Exits 1* and *2* also fell into the hands of paras, the men of Colonel Sink's *506th Parachute Infantry Regiment,* who had landed on *Drop Zone C.* Lieutenant-Colonel Strayer secured *Exit 2* while Major-General Taylor in person led the columns Turner and Ewell towards *Exit 1 and* Pouppeville. Contact was established with the *4th US ID,* who had landed on *Utah Beach*. The *101st Airborne* had accomplished its mission.

4th US Infantry Division « Ivy Division »

The *4th US ID*, placed under the orders of Major-General Barton, was a unit which had prepared meticulously for D-Day. The many amphibious training exercises which they undertook proved essential. Nevertheless, in April 1944, German motor torpedo boats surprised a convoy during the exercise *Tiger*, causing heavy losses in human lives.

Its objective was to land on the east coast of the Cotentin Peninsula, north of the Baie des Veys. The sandy beach was ideal, but the hinterland was swampy and, moreover, dominated by hills. The support of airborne forces was therefore essential to secure control of the beach exits. If *Utah* remained separate from the rest of the bridgehead, as long as Carentan was not taken, the *Overlord* planners calculated that the town could become an essential starting-point for the conquest of Cherbourg.

A GI of the 4th US ID on Utah Beach. Unlike the soldiers landing on Omaha, he wore Uniform Model 43, impregnated with an anti-gas product. On his chest, gas mask M5 in its rubber case, specially designed for D-Day. At the waist, a lifebelt, different from the airborne troops' Mae West which certainly could not be worn on the belt for fear of tipping head-first into the water and not being able to re-emerge, because of the weight of equipment.

Coll. T. Le Sant

A column of the 4th US ID goes up in line before *Cobra*. The soldier in the foreground is an NCO, recognisable by the horizontal white line painted on the rear of his helmet. After the hell of the hedges, it was time for the breakthrough! NARA

Spared on D-Day, the division was rapidly confronted by particularly tenacious enemy resistance. Continuing their operations in Normandy was now proving more difficult for Barton's men. The German defence of Quinéville and Montebourg, as well as of the batteries at Azeville and Crisbecq represented a serious setback. The tenacity of the opponent was such that Major-General Collins, the leader of the *7th US Corps*, decided to proceed first with cutting off the Cotentin peninsula, before mounting an attack on Cherbourg, whose capture was absolutely vital in terms of logistics. The *4th US ID* contributed to the surrender of the great port before the unit was redeployed towards the south.

GIs dug a trench in the shelter of the anti-tank wall which ran along Utah Beach. For the 4th US ID, the worst fighting was yet to come ...
Caen Memorial

Losses in the month of June amounted to 5,452 men; 4,400 recruits came to fill the depleted ranks. The month of July gave the unit no rest, because difficult fighting over the *bocage* awaited the division from July 7 onwards. The *GIs* of the *4th US ID* faced the *Fallschirmjäger* and the *SS*, entrenched on the heights as well as in a maze of hedges on the Périers road. Six hundred men were lost on the first day of the offensive, for insignificant gains. As well as facing a tenacious defence, the Americans were handicapped by the marshes, the mud, and especially the hedgerows. On July 15, bled dry - 2,300 men had been lost, including many officers - the division was placed in reserve.

Ivy was the emblem of the 4th US ID. The symbol is a play on words in English, Ivy being also the two letters I and V, or 4 in Roman numerals.
Coll. T. Le Sant

The *4th US ID* having behaved admirably under fire, it was chosen to participate in *Operation Cobra.* It seized La Chapelle-en-Juger on July 26, then Villedieu-les-Poêles on August 1, before supporting the *30th US ID,* severely stretched during the German counter-attack on Mortain. At the end of August, the division was granted the honour of participating - albeit in a somewhat overshadowed way - in the liberation of Paris, at the side of Leclerc's 2nd DB.

Throughout the autumn, the *4th US ID* was engaged in the terrible fighting in the forest of Hürtgen. Sent to rest in the Ardennes, a sector believed to be at peace, it was faced with the German counter-offensive in the winter of 1944 -1945. In March 1945, after the passage of the Rhine, the unit pressed on to the heart of Bavaria, and finished the war in Miesbach.

UTAH BEACH

On June 6, 1944, in fact, the *4th US ID* landed on *Utah Beach,* a few kilometres further south than planned because of the currents which caused the first assault barges to drift. Brigadier-General Roosevelt, second-in-command of the division, believed that this error - a fortunate one, since the beaches originally chosen were actually much better fortified than the sector on which the landings took place - was of no consequence. At 08:00, the *8th Infantry Regiment* was fully landed. Supported by 22 *DD* tanks out of the 32 launched at sea, the *GIs* quickly secured the beach, which remained held despite being the target of sporadic shelling. The landing was a success, and its joining up with the airborne forces was carried out by the middle of the same day. Losses only amounted to 197 men on *Utah Beach,* of which 60 were lost at sea, and only 118 men, including 12 killed, in the first two infantry regiments who were engaged. In addition, the *Naval Combat Demolition Unit* and the sappers of *the Beach Obstacle Demolition Party* announced the loss of 60 men.

A 105 mm gun belonging to the 4th US ID in the heat of battle. The artillery was a trump card for the US Army, being able to carry out TOT (Time On Target) coordinated fire of at least a regiment. NARA

Soldiers of the medical corps give first aid to the wounded on Utah Beach. The losses were limited to fewer than 200 men, but immediate treatment was necessary to save those still alive. NARA (© Editions Ouest-France - colorisation Graph&ti)

29th US Infantry Division « Blue and Grey »

A GI of the 29th US ID, surrounded by crates of equipment of all kinds: medical equipment, rations ... D-Day required meticulous logistics in order to support the assault waves.
Coll. T. Le Sant

The *29th US ID* is a division of the National Guard, that is to say the State militia, and not of the *US Army*, which is the regular army. The command of the *29th US ID* was assumed by the impatient and aggressive Major-General Gerhardt, an officer very strong on discipline; certainly respected, but loathed by many. On the eve of D-Day, the men, well trained, were confident, but very few had ever experienced enemy fire.

The insignia of the 29th US ID 'Blue and Grey', reminiscent of the Yin-Yang symbol, and indicating that the units in this group of the National Guard came from both the Southern and Northern States of the USA.
Coll. T. Le Sant

The *29th US ID* had to lead the attack on Saint-Laurent-sur-Mer and Vierville-sur-Mer, at *Omaha Beach*. On D-Day, a 15-knot wind and currents made navigation difficult, and the landing craft were struggling with 1.5 metre waves. Many of the *GIs* suffered from seasickness, were chilled to the bone and soaked through. They had to cover several hundred metres under hellish fire to hope to reach the seawall. A thousand men were lost by this single *116th Regiment*, which was a third of the task force. For the lack of help, many of the wounded died on the beach or perished, drowned by the rising tide; radio equipment was lost; there was insufficient support from armoured personnel carriers; and with no assault corridors opened by the engineers, the American soldiers remain in an impasse, in the face of a virtually intact German defence, for a long time. Success was finally achieved thanks to the courage and pugnacity of a few groups of infantry, and the support of the fleet. On D-Day, 1,342 men were lost by the *29th US ID* and the units which were attached to it. On June 11, their right flank joined up with the troops of the *101st Airborne:* there was, however, only one single bridgehead in Normandy.

Progress southwards was in the face of a pugnacious adversary. Because of this, on June 12, 224 men were lost. By June 13, losses already stood at 2,440 men. The 'Hedgerows War' which ensued during the entire month of June and the first half of July bled the division dry, as its young, inexperienced soldiers discover the hell of the war in the *bocage*. Faced with the *Fallschirmjäger* and the *SS*, the 'Hedgerows War' which led the division toward Saint-Lô, was very costly. On July 18, a *Task Force* led by General Cota finally seized Saint-Lô. This battle was the most costly of the entire conflict for the *Blue and Grey Division*. They had lost 7,000 men - of whom more than 2,000 had died - since D-Day.

CARNAGE ON *DOG GREEN*

06:35 The *GIs* of company A of the *1st Battalion, 116th Infantry Regiment,* were greeted by a hail of fire which was unleashed as soon as the ramps of their LCAs were lowered. Many were forced to jump overboard, and to seek a precarious shelter in the water behind obstacles on the beach. The wounded were drowned by the rising tide. Most of those who risked venturing on to the beach were shot down. In just ten minutes, the unit lost all its officers and sub-officers. Three quarters of the two hundred men of the company were killed or injured. For the handful of survivors, exhausted and in a state of shock, the hell of *Omaha* had only just begun.

The *29th US ID* resumed the offensive on July 29 and found itself heavily engaged, particularly in the Percy sector, where it repelled a vain German counter-attack. Equally heavy fighting awaited them on the Vire road, before finally being withdrawn from the front for some time on August 15. The conduct of the division under fire was admirable, but the losses were such that by the month of August, the division was no longer the same as that which had landed on the morning of June 6.

After the Normandy breakthrough, the *29th US ID* was engaged in Brittany, and participated in the siege of Brest up to its surrender in mid-September. Engaged in the terrible fighting toward the Roer in the autumn, the division crossed the Rhine in 1945 and took part in the cleaning-up operation of the Ruhr pocket. On May 4, it was in position on the River Elbe.

On June 6, for the GIs of the 29th US ID and the troops of the engineers which were attached to it, it was 'Bloody Omaha'.
Mémorial de Caen

The 29th US ID had to fight hard for a month and a half to open the Saint-Lô road. The apprenticeship in the Hedgerows War was very hard, and costly in human lives. The man with the Colt 45 is carrying a handie-talkie on his left shoulder.
NARA

1st US Infantry Division « Big Red One »

Soldiers of the 'Big Red One' landed in Normandy dressed in the 1941-style jacket, the standard cotton uniform. All the men had an M5 gas mask. The NCOs were usually armed with a Thompson sub-machine gun, as here, or an M3 Grease Gun.
Musée de Colleville-sur-Mer

The *1st US ID* followed an excellent, continual training programme from 1940 onwards, well before the entry of the United States into the war. It took part in *Operation Torch* in North Africa, then in the Tunisia campaign, before leading a second landing in Sicily. Because of the unit's experience, it was chosen to carry out the assault on *D-Day*

Sections of the Assault Boat Teams each comprised a group with an M1A1 bazooka. This weapon proved very useful to neutralise German positions by sending projectiles through openings in the bunkers. This man is wearing a gas detection armband.
Musée de Colleville-sur-Mer

After D-Day, the 'Big Red One' reached Caumont-L'Eventé in a week: this was the furthest advance over the whole of the bridgehead. Coll. T. Le Sant

under the command of Major-General Huebner, an energetic officer and a true leader of men. Its operational capacities were far from being usurped, and the intensive training which it underwent in view of D-Day made it a division meticulously prepared for its task. However, since 1942, the members of the division had felt a sense of superiority with regard to other units of the *US Army*, and felt they had the right to request special treatment.

The first wave landed on *Omaha* at 06:30. The intensity of the fighting and the carnage which ensued gave this landing sector the nickname of *Bloody Omaha*. However, supported by a powerful fleet, the tenacity of the *GIs* prevailed and, with difficulty, the bridgehead was established. The immediate result of the Battle of Normandy was, however, substantially easier for the *Big Red One* since the advance towards the south seemed inexorable, and was carried out at little cost. It also seized Caumont-l'Éventé, on the morning of June 13. In one week, it recorded 1,744 losses, but captured 600 prisoners on one day, June 9. At the beginning of July, the division was stuck in the *bocage* before taking part in *Operation Cobra* on July 25, during the exploitation phase. Huebner, together with the *CCB* of the *3rd US Armored Division*, went through the gap made by the *9th US ID* and seized Marigny on July 27. The irresistible advance then continued, because the enemy no longer seemed able to re-establish itself on new defences. Brécey was reached on July 31. The *1st US ID* then took part in the encircling manoeuvre which led to the formation of the Falaise Pocket. The fighting, however, remained very fierce, in the face of a determined enemy. Striking first towards the south-east, towards Mayenne, the division then went back northwards and fought the Germans at the south of the Pocket. On August 24, it was at Chartres. The Seine was crossed two days later, at Corbeil and Melun.

Infantry soldiers of the 1st US ID. The motorised 'Big Red One' played a leading part in *Operation Cobra*, which led to the decisive breakthrough. Archives du Calvados

An MP in a jeep fitted with a fording kit, that is to say a device allowing it to get to the beach from a landing barge without the vehicle's engine being flooded by sea water. Note the plastic cover which protects the individual weapon, typical of D-Day. Behind the star-spangled banner fixed to the windscreen, the checklist for de-waterproofing the vehicle. NARA

THE HELL OF *OMAHA BEACH*

The landing at *Omaha Beach* was very much more difficult than expected. The naval and air bombardments had failed, and the assault was carried out in the worst conditions, and in the face of powerful, undamaged coastal defences. The currents and enemy fire prevented the pilots of the *LCVPs* to maintain their course and many units did not reach land in the planned beach area. The men, overloaded with equipment, landed under a hail of bullets and shells, in cold, deep water. Twenty-seven *Sherman DDs* out of thirty-two sank in the rough sea, depriving the *Big Red One* of their valuable support. The first success came on the left wing when Lieutenant Cutler managed to seize *WN 60,* with the support of the destroyer *Doyle*. From 8 o'clock onwards, the *GIs* began to cross the seawall located at the height of the present-day cemetery. The fighting towards the hinterland was also very fierce, due to their failure to open the beach exits quickly for the vehicles congregating on the beach. On the evening of June 6, the assault regiment, the *16th RCT,* registered the loss of 962 men. The total losses of the division and the units which were attached to it amounted to 1,347 men. On June 7th, 4,842 men were lost in the *Omaha* sector. By the evening of June 6, the essential had been achieved: the bridgehead was narrow, but five regiments had landed.

The *Big Red One* was involved in all the *1st US Army's* major combats. It was they who seized Aix-la-Chapelle, the first important German town conquered by the Allies. After that, they fought in difficult conditions in the forest of Hürtgen, then in the Ardennes. After having fought in the Ruhr, they finished the war in Czechoslovakia.

D-Day, H-Hour, Easy Red, on June 6. The coastal zone visible on the photograph is the present location of the American Cemetery. Mémorial de Caen

In a few moments these GIs of the 'Big Red One' would be plunged into the hell of Omaha. Officers were recognisable by the vertical bar painted on the back of their helmets. On the right, standing up with a lifejacket, a sailor of the Coast Guards. The men, suffering from sea-sickness, were plunged into anxiety and extreme tension: the fateful moment was near.
NARA (© Editions Ouest-France - colorisation Graph&ti)

The badge of the 1st US ID 'Big Red One'.
Coll. T. Le Sant

A GMC: a lorry typical of the high degree of motorisation of the US Army. Coll. T. Le Sant

50th British Infantry Division « Northumbrian »

Major-General Graham's *50th Northumbrian Division* was a territorial division at the opening of hostilities in 1939. After the 1940 campaign, it operated in the Middle East and then in North Africa, where it suffered substantial losses. It made its first landing in Sicily. On its return to Great Britain in 1943, the division, designated for D-Day, prepared intensively for the amphibious assault. The *50th Northumbrian Division* was given the task of leading the assault on *Gold Beach*, located 15 kilometres to the east of *Omaha Beach*, where the Americans with whom Graham was to join forces would land on D-Day. The division embarked on June 3 in Portsmouth, after having received a visit from the Prime Minister, Winston Churchill.

The insignia of the 50th ID forming two Ts and an H, for the three Northumbrian rivers: Tyne, Tees and Humber. Coll. T. Le Sant

An infantry soldier of the 50th ID. The pouches, these broad cartridge pouches which gave the Tommy his typical silhouette, could take a lot of equipment, including Bren gun magazines. The man also carries clips for his Lee-Enfield NO. 4 MkI in a light cartridge belt over his shoulder. Coll. T. Le Sant

Twenty-five thousand men came ashore on *Gold* on June 6. There were 413 losses on the beaches. The division had the honour of being the only unit to have obtained a *Victoria Cross* on this historic day, the prestigious decoration being awarded to Sergeant Major Hollis of the *6th Green Howards*. Although contact was made with the Canadians, they did not join up with the Americans.

On June 10, the *50th Northumbrian Division* participated in *Operation Perch* and faced the *Panzer Lehr* in the Lingevres sector. The *8th Armoured Brigade* fought at its side. The Hedgerows War was a severe setback for the veterans of the desert and Sicily. Inter-service co-ordination suffered. On June 17, the division managed to seize Tilly-sur-Seulles after strenuous infantry combat, but the next day, it was thrown back again with the loss of Hottot-les-Bagues. On June 24, it suffered another failure before Hottot and Juvigny-sur-Seulles, in the context of *Operation Martlet*.

The landing on Gold Beach, here from LCIs equipped with their characteristic side openings, took place overall without major difficulties. The first waves arrived aboard LCAs. IWM

GOLD BEACH

H Hour was fixed at 07:25. The landing fleet came under attack by the Longues battery, but three of the four guns were quickly reduced to silence. On the beach near le Hamel, the *1st Hampshire* progressed slowly and the engineers suffered the greatest difficulties. The German defenders, outmanoeuvred, did not cease fighting until 16:00. At les Roquettes, the *1st Dorset* experienced fewer difficulties in crossing the beach. To the east of *Gold Beach,* on *King Beach,* two battalions, the *6th Green Howards* and *5th East Yorkshire,* reduced the German defences, thanks to the presence of tanks and the effectiveness of the naval support. The clean-up of the fortified houses in La Rivière, however, required a fierce struggle. Several batteries were silenced and progress continued towards Crépon and Creully. The commandos of the *47th Royal Marine,* on the other hand, had fallen behind: Port-en-Bessin was not taken on D-Day. At the beginning of the afternoon, all of the *50th Division* had landed, and could begin the operation of getting into a good position to seize Bayeux the following day.

The landings on Gold Beach were much less bloody than those on Omaha. The Germans, however, fought with both energy and despair. The warship in the centre, ramps down, is an LCT which was capable of landing several tanks. The soldiers, on the other and, disembarked on a small LCA-type barge. IWM

The unit then experienced a period of relative calm up to its involvement in *Operation Bluecoat* with the *30th British Corps*. The division did not exactly shine on this occasion. Its progress was one of the slowest, although it only faced weak counter-attacks by the *272.ID*. It liberated Villers-Bocage on August 4 and Conde-sur-Noireau on August 16, not without having faced fierce resistance. Graham's men then put pressure on the north wing of the Falaise Pocket. The *Northumbrians* finally passed the Seine between August 25 and 28. Of the three veteran divisions of the fighting in North Africa, the other two being

The Sexton, a self-propelled ordnance QF 25 pounder gun on an RAM chassis (a Canadian-made tank), brought mobility to the British artillery regiments. Coll. T. Le Sant

Photo souvenir for a few comrades. Note the different hairstyles and uniforms. The man in the first row on the right is wearing a leather jerkin, reminiscent of the First World War. Coll. T. Le Sant

Some villages seem to have been spared by the fighting. Everywhere, even where the houses were no more than rubble, the British were greeted with relief by most of the Normans. IWM

the *7th British Armoured Division* and the *51st Highland Division*, the *50th Northumbrian Division* is regarded as having been the most effective during the Battle of Normandy.

The unit resumed combat duties in Belgium, then especially in Holland, during *Operation Market Garden*. The war stopped prematurely that autumn for the *50th Northumbrian*. In the face of the staff crisis which affected the British army, Marshal Montgomery was compelled to dissolve the unit, much to the chagrin of the Prime Minister, Winston Churchill.

3rd Canadian Infantry Division

Formed in 1940, Major-General Keller's *3rd Canadian ID* was selected from the month of June 1943, to take part in the initial assault of *Overlord*. Preparations for the Battle of Normandy were focused on the techniques of amphibious assault, to the particular detriment of co-operation with the *2nd Canadian Armoured Brigade*, which was attached to it.

While some German positions put up a tenacious defence, the landing on *Juno Beach* was a success. Although the rendez-vous took place that day with the British forces who had landed on *Gold*, the congestion on the beaches had caused delays, so access between *Juno and Sword* was maintained with difficulty. Moreover, the Carpiquet airfield had not been taken.

A Canadian signals soldier with a portable radio device. These portable walkie-talkies were essential to ensure good troop coordination. The Canadian uniform was similar in every way to the British one, only the fabric was rather more green. Coll. T. Le Sant

A Canadian is receiving first aid outside Carpiquet, near a wall behind which three infantrymen are sheltering, ready to open fire; part of the wall has collapsed, either over the years or as the result of firing, which improves their cover. They had to fight for a month before finally seizing Carpiquet and its airfield. PAC

This photograph was taken on Juno Beach on June 6, probably during the evening as the weather is sunny. A temporary road has been laid down to keep them from becoming bogged down in the sand. The engineers have also taken the time to pile up the beach defences before destroying them. On the right is a Bren Carrier, still fitted with the extra plates fixed to the edges of its body to prevent it from taking on water while disembarking. The special patterns used to camouflage the ships by breaking up their silhouettes can also be seen.
NARA

Over the following days, it bore the brunt of the deadly counter-attack of the *12.SS Panzer.* The ferocity of the fighting between these two units was very costly in human lives. Four hundred and twenty men, and twenty-eight tanks, were lost at Buron on June 7. In addition, war crimes were perpetrated during the confrontation. Progress toward Caen was therefore halted. It was only thanks to *Operation Windsor,* from July 4-9, that the Canadians finally managed to take over their D-Day goal, Carpiquet Airport. They also took part in the liberation of the left bank of Caen

JUNO BEACH

On D-Day, the *3rd Canadian* landed between Saint-Aubin-sur-Mer and Courseulles-sur-Mer. The enemy was determined, and the fighting fierce. In Saint-Aubin, a fortified position established around a 50 mm gun fell only after a long and costly battle. On the other wing, on *Mike Red* to the west of Courseulles, *B Company* of the *Royal Winnipeg Rifles* lost 133 men and had no more than 27 able-bodied combatants left. The day however was to the Canadians. Losses amounted to 1,200 men on *Juno Beach,* including 319 killed, 528 wounded and 45 taken prisoner. Progress was then slowed only by a few pockets of resistance, which were formidable. At Fontaine-Henry, six *Shermans* were burned by shots from 88mm guns. The German front was very weakly held, but the Canadians were not in a position to take advantage of this. The next day, the *3rd Canadian* faced the *Hitlerjügend,* who had just reached the front line.

A Centaur tank. Fitted with a 95mm howitzer, it was used in the Royal Marines' armoured support sections.
Photo. T. Le Sant

French civilians of Bernières-sur-Mer grouped around the Norman House, still standing today: they feared snipers. PAC

The badge of the 3rd Canadian Division: a simple grey-blue rectangle. Coll. T. Le Sant

(Operation Charnwood). As proof of the intensity of the struggle and the sacrifices made, 4,584 men had been killed or injured since June 6. The division freed the suburb of Vaucelles, on the right bank of the Orne, the factory at Colombelles and Cormelles le Royal in the context of *Operation Atlantic*, triggered on July 18.

On July 25, the division once again launched an assault. This was *Operation Spring*. The fighting for Tilly-la-Campagne was, however, very costly in the face of the skilful and determined *SS* defenders. All their gains had to be abandoned. The *2nd Canadian Corps* suffered 1,500 losses on July 25, including 570 men killed. Fighting resumed over the following days, and only resulted in additional losses for negligible territorial gains. On August 1 and the following night, several unsuccessful assaults were also launched on Tilly-la-Campagne.

The *3rd Canadian ID* was relieved from July 30 onwards. Its rehabilitation period was of short duration since, on August 9, it was involved in *Operation Totalize*. It was, however, only involved at the second level and seized Hill 206, overlooking Potigny, as well as Hill195, and fought in the woods of Quesnay. The continuation of the offensive during the *Operation Tractable* once again caused significant losses during the laborious progress of pushing back the *Kampfgruppe Krause* of the *Hitlerjügend*. On August 21, it was in the sector of Trun, then headed for Rouen, reaching it on August 29.

From September 10 until October 1 1944, the *3rd Canadian ID* crushed the pockets of Boulogne and then Calais. After that, it fought in Belgium and then the Netherlands, where it was involved in difficult battles until 1945. At the end of the war, it penetrated into Germany and captured the port of Emden.

The la Chaudière regiment of the 8th Brigade, whose members were French Canadian, which surprised the Norman civilians.
Coll. T. Le Sant

Rots, June 15 1944. Corporal Castailloux, a motorcycle despatch rider of La Chaudière's regiment, is being shown which route to follow by an MP, Sergeant Giles. The Divisions included a considerable number of non-combattants, essential to keep them battle-ready. PAC

These Shermans, of Fort Garry Horse's A Squadron, had been burned out near the church in Rots. The first battles against the Hitlerjungend resulted in the loss of dozens of Shermans and hundreds of men. PAC

3rd British Infantry Division, « Iron Division »

A soldier of the 3rd ID in battle dress. The battle-dress blouse had an unfortunate tendency to uncover the lower back, while the gaiters, too small, did not stay properly in place.
Coll. T. Le Sant

This active unit took part in the 1940 campaign under the orders of an officer who went on to play a leading role during the conflict: Bernard Law Montgomery. After four years in England under the command of Major-General Rennie, it was designated to take part in the Normandy landings on *Sword Beach*. Its mission was to ensure a solid bridgehead, and then to occupy Caen.

They had to shelter from machine-gun fire against the vehicles immobilised on the beach. The bottleneck on the foreshore caused serious, long delays and contributed to making it impossible to take Caen on June 6. The 40 mm Bofors in the background had proved impossible to install in the battery, and the fascines had been abandoned on the shore, probably by a Churchill AVRE.
IWM

SWORD BEACH

The assault was led by the *8th Brigade,* which landed at 07:30. The terribly effective bombing crushed the enemy defences and pockets of resistance were reduced by the action of the *Funnies*. The fighting was, however, fierce in some sectors. Six hundred and thirty men were lost on the beaches. The bottleneck caused by this, however, caused considerable delays. In addition, the *3rd British ID* lost precious time in consolidating the bridgehead. It was also delayed by the opposing defence: the fortified site *Hillman,* on the road to Caen, held up the *1st Suffolk Regiment* for ten hours! This delay prevented the rapid engagement of the *185th Brigade,* which waited until the *8th* opened the road to Caen. In addition, the *9th Brigade* was sent in support of the *6th Airborne* to the east of the Orne, instead to intervene on the right flank, in the direction of *Juno Beach,* as had been originally planned. This excessive caution and the accumulated delays gave the *21.Panzers* time to build up the German disposition to the north of Caen and to prevent the progress of the *3rd ID*.

The landing met with major opposition on the beaches; the capital of Lower Normandy was not reached; and the division marked time for a month outside the city. The fighting for the Château de la Londe and around the wood of Lébisey were costly. By the morning of June 8, the *3rd British account ID* had already suffered 996 losses. On June 13, Rennie, wounded, was temporarily replaced at the head of the division by Brigadier Cass, who took interim charge until Major-General Whistler assumed command. By July 1, the losses since D-Day amounted to 3,508 men. By the same date, the division had collected 53,143 tonnes of provisioning

The Ordnance QF 25 Pounder, almost 90 mm, was the workhorse of the British field artillery. There were 72 per division.
Photo T. Le Sant

Caen was finally liberated on July 8, thanks to *Operation Charnwood,* a major operation launched by the *2nd British Army.* Six hundred and thirty-two guns and seventy-eight large guns from the Royal Navy were placed at the disposal of the *1st British Corps* to support the assault. Eighty thousand shells were fired in front of Caen during the five days preceding the attack. Five hundred tanks supported the infantry units. On July 7, the operation started with an aerial bombardment which crushed the northern part of the city. This bombardment finished at 23:00, but the British troops did not stop the assault until 04:20 on the following day, July 8. The Germans, of course, turned this delay to their advantage. The timid advance of the British was, furthermore, handicapped by the multitude of craters which slowed down their progress. Because of the ruins accumulated in the city and the delaying actions of a few groups of the enemy rearguard, the allied advance was slow but at 13:00, the bridges of Orne, which had been destroyed, were taken by men from the *3rd British ID,* who had finally achieved their D-Day objectives.

The badge of the 3rd ID 'Iron Division': the triangular shape symbolises the '3' of the division, and its three infantry regiments.
Coll. T. Le Sant

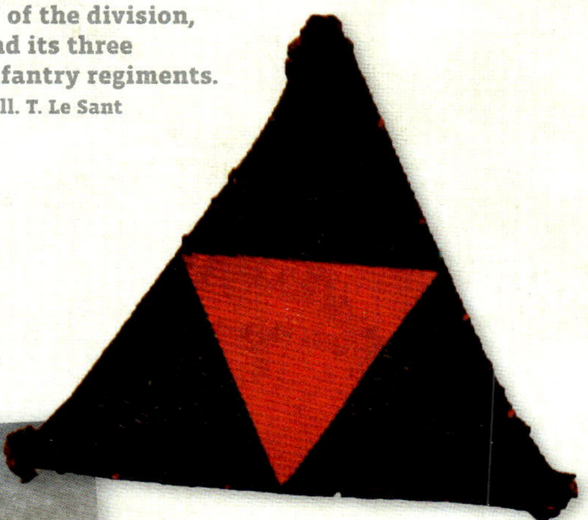

08:45, White Beach sector. Sappers (distinguished by a painted strip on their helmets) and medical orderlies have just set foot on Sword Beach. The kit is particularly impressive. The assault jacket adopted in 1942 can be seen on the soldiers in the foreground.
IWM (© Editions Ouest-France - colorisation Graph&ti)

In Caen, French civilians with a liberator, probably at the door of their home, which seems to have suffered some damage. The British soldiers became aware of the price of freedom when they saw the devastated Norman towns, and were filled with admiration at the warm welcome they were given.
Coll. T. Le Sant

The division then moved to the east of the Orne, in the airborne bridgehead. In this way it took part in the support attacks of *Operation Goodwood*, launched toward the crest of Bourguébus. At the beginning of August, the division faced the enemy in the Bény-Bocage - Flers sector. The losses are considerable on August 10, when it suffered the shock of a counter-attack by the *10.SS Panzerdivision*. The courage of Corporal Sidney Bates during this confrontation at Chênedollé was rewarded by the granting of a posthumous *Victoria Cross*.

The division was then placed at rest with the *8th British Corps* until mid-September, the date on which it was again engaged in Holland In 1945, the division took part in the Rhineland campaign, crossed the Rhine and finished the war in Bremen.

Les Funnies de la 79th Armoured Division

A British tank crewman of the 79th Armoured Division. He wears the characteristic helmet of armoured units as well as a holster for drawing his revolver more easily when in a sitting position.
Coll. T. Le Sant

The bull's head, emblem of the 79th Armoured Division

The supposed strength of the Atlantic Wall defences and the obstacles of all kinds accumulated on the beaches led the British to a huge tactical innovation for D-Day*:* the massive employment of specialised armoured cars. These *Funnies* were developed within Major-General Hobart's *79th Armoured Division*. The talent of his team had allowed them to achieve these timely innovations.

The medium-sized *Sherman* tank served as the basis for two variants. The *Sherman Crab* or *Flail* was a mine clearance machine. The mine clearance system actually consisted of a rotating drum fitted with chains attached to the front of the body. Three hundred *Crabs* were ordered at the end of 1943. The *Sherman Duplex Drive* - or *DD* - was in fact an amphibious tank. Propellers and a system of folding canvas skirts allowed the 35 tonne armoured car to float at approximately 9 km/h on a reasonably calm sea. Five hundred of these devices were ordered.

A Churchill AVRE 'Petard' at Bernières-sur-Mer on June 6. The intervention of the 'Funnies' from General Hobart's menagerie was decisive on the Anglo-Canadian beaches, saving many human lives.
Mémorial de Caen

The second tank used was the *Churchill*. The *AVRE* variant consisted of a transformation of the armament, replacing the gun with a powerful 290 mm mortar (*the Petard*), which was capable of quickly levelling reinforced concrete and was designed to strike bunker embrasures and anti-tank walls. It could also be fitted with fascines and a mobile bridge to allow for crossing obstacles such as ditches or water courses. Seven hundred tank conversions were requested. Nearly 200 *AVRE* equipped

THE *DUPLEX DRIVE* ON *D-DAY*

In addition to the entire *27th Armoured Brigade,* six regiments - three American, two Canadian and another British - were equipped with *Sherman DDs.* If the *DDs* had to be jettisoned off *Gold* because of the state of the sea, at *Sword,* 34 *DDs* were put into the water and 31 arrived on the beach, ten minutes after the other *Funnies.* On *Juno,* the situation was more complicated, because 19 *DDs* out of the 38 launched at sea sank under the waves. But the worst disaster occurred on *Omaha:* 24 out of 29 sank, the other 5 being rapidly destroyed on the beach. On *Utah,* everything worked out for the best since 27 of the 28 *DDs* put into the water reached the shore. Out of the 129 *DDs* launched at sea on June 6, 47 sank before reaching the coast. As for the other *Funnies,* the contribution of the *Sherman DDs* proved crucial to the success of D-Day, including on Omaha Beach where, if the commitment of the machines brought by *LCT* directly on to the beach was not sufficient to ensure victory, it contributed to turn round a poorly committed situation for the Americans.

The Sherman Crab or Flail, of which 300 were ordered, had an ingenious system - a rotating drum fitted with chaines - to cause the mines to explode. PAC

three of the assault regiments. The *Churchill Ark I*, which was only a chassis without a turret, also took the place of a bridge. To guard against a beach surface which was too soft, a variant, named *Bobbin*, operated by laying a carpet which could unroll in front of the tank on the sand. Finally, the *Churchill Crocodile* was a terrifying flamethrower tank. Two hundred and fifty were ordered, but only three were involved on June 6, 1944.

The Churchill AVRE 'Petard' at Courseulles-sur-Mer was one of the 200 with which the assault waves were equipped. It had a 290 mm mortar, intended to neutralise bunkers. Photo T. Le Sant

A Crab crew.
Armoured vehicles remained the favourite target for anti-tank guns: these men needed a lot of courage on D-Day. Coll. T. Le Sant

A Humber scout-car of the 30th Armoured Brigade, belonging to the 79th Armoured Division, at Beuville in the Caen plain on July 8 1944, the day of *Operation Charnwood*, which finally allowed the left bank of the devastated town to be taken. The officer who is surveying the ground is Brigadier Duncan. The number 50 on his machine indicates that he is the staff officer of an armoured brigade. IWM

A Sherman amphibious Duplex Drive, preserved at Courseulles-sur-Mer but without its 'skirts'. Five hundred of these devices were ordered for the six regiments thrown into the assault of the Atlantikwall. Coll. T. Le Sant

Commandos

The shoulder and sleeve insignia of the commando units.
Coll. T. Le Sant

The British were the specialists of small, highly trained formations operating rapid strikes against the enemy. Operations were conducted in France, from 1940 onwards, then in Norway and the Mediterranean from 1941. The most daring raids were those on Saint-Nazaire and Dieppe in 1942. Two brigades of commandos disembarked on June 6, 1944: the *1st* and *4th Service Special Brigades* . Lord Lovat's *1st Special Service Brigade* was composed of 2,500 men, including his personal piper Bill Millin, and included the *No. 4 Commando*, originally formed of volunteers from 85 different units. Commanded by Lieutenant-Colonel Dawson, this battalion was added to by the men of *No. 10 Commando*, Allied Unit, namely 177 Frenchmen from the 1st BFMC (Marine Commando Battalion) of the Free French Naval Forces, commanded by Commander Kieffer.

A commando, wearing the famous green beret. He is armed with the no less famous Thompson sub-machine gun, called the Tommy Gun: an effective weapon for short-range fighting. Like the paras, the commandos each carried a toggle rope on D-Day. Coll. T. Le Sant

This famous photograph, taken at Bénouville, illustrates the contact effected by the commandos landing on Sword and the airborne troops. These last, recognisable by their caps and their Denison Smoke camouflage smocks, were exhausted: the relief did not arrive until after they had fought for more than ten hours. The commando in the front row is carrying the rucksack typical of D-Day for units who had to move forward without logistical support. IWM

The *1st Special Service Brigade* landed on *Sword* and seized its objectives at Riva-Bella and Ouistreham with *No. 4 Commando* while the bulk of the brigade met up with the airborne forces at Bénouville. *No. 41 Royal Marine Commando*, for its part, landed to the west of *Sword* but, held up by heavy losses, was unable to join forces with *No. 48 Royal Navy* which had landed on *Juno*, where it suffered 50% losses for insignificant results. *No. 47 Royal Marine Commando* landed on *Gold Beach*, bypassed Arromanches and seized Port-en-Bessin, its D-Day objective, on June 8 after a day of fierce fighting. On the morning of June 7, the losses of the two commando brigades amounted to 659 men.

While *No. 46 Royal Marine Commando* was engaged in the valley of the Mue, on June 17,

Commandos of Lord Lovat's 1st Special Service Brigade at Colleville-sur-Orne. They had to head inland to lend a hand to the airborne troops. IWM

An M5 Stuart tank, preserved in the Musée du Grand Bunker in Ouistreham. Photo T. Le Sant

No. 41 Royal Marine Commando finally managed to take over the Douvres-la-Délivrande radar station. The two *Special Service Brigades* reinforced the airborne bridgehead on the right bank of the Orne and carried on a difficult war of positions . The clashes around Bavent wood on fixed positions were reminiscent of the trench warfare of the previous conflict. On August 1, the heights on the Dozulé road were taken by the commandos, who managed to infiltrate them during the night. These men were then involved in *Operation Paddle*, which took the British to the Seine by liberating the Auge area.

The talents of commandos were needed again on several occasions before the end of the war, particularly on the island of Walcheren in autumn 1944, and during the crossing of the Rhine in March 1945.

Three army commando units landed on June 6: the No. 3, 4, and 6 Commandos. Coll. T. Le Sant

The commando units were formed in 1940 on the express orders of Churchill. The Old Lion had already foreseen the return to the continent. In the meantime, they had to harass the enemy by launching raids on the European coast. IWM

British propaganda made every effort to maintain public morale: commando squads launched raids on the enemy, forcing them to maintain a large garrison in Norway throughout the conflict. Private collection.

These commandos, recognisable by their berets and shoulder insignia, belong to Troop 3 of No. 3 Commando. They are overloaded with supplies and equipment on this day, June 6, including the essential lifebelts and stretchers. In the background can be seen the temporary gangway of a Churchill AVRE. IWM

Five marine commando units taking part in D-Day: the No. 41, 45, 46, 47 and 48 Royal Marine Commandos.
Coll. T. Le Sant

1ST BFMC AT RIVA-BELLA

The first commandos to disembark on *Sword* at 07:31 were the French of the 1st BFMC. An *LCI* bore the brunt, and a hail of lead welcomed the commandos to the beach, on which forty of them were mown down. Many bunkers were cleared out, but the resistance around the key position of the casino was tough. It took the intervention of a *Sherman DD* brought in by Commander Kieffer to end it. At 11:30, their mission accomplished, the French commandos returned to a point near a holiday village to collect their packs and continued their progress inland, in the footsteps of Lord Lovat who was marching on *Pegasus Bridge*. The 1st BFMC lost fifty-five men on June 6.

Rangers

The *Rangers*, the American commandos, were the elite soldiers. They were the first *GIs to* be engaged in a land combat in Europe, since fifty of them took part in the raid on Dieppe before fighting in the Mediterranean. On June 6, 1944, the *2nd* and *5th Rangers Battalions* formed the *Provisional Ranger Group*, placed under the command of Lieutenant-Colonel Rudder.

Force A, made up of 225 men of the *2nd Rangers*, had to climb the cliff at the Pointe du Hoc and destroy the artillery pieces which were there. Rudder was considerably delayed, and the assault did not begin until 07:10, making it impossible for it to be reinforced by the *5th Rangers* who, unable to be contacted, headed for *Omaha* . The goal was reached, however, although Rudder's isolated position remained very precarious. *Force B*, then *Force C*, came ashore on *Omaha.* Captain Goranson's *Force B* (a company) managed to proceed rapidly to the top of the cliffs at the Pointe de la Percée, on the right flank of *Omaha.* The entry into the field of the *5th Rangers* (Lieutenant-Colonel Schneider's *C Force*) contributed to the success of the day, in spite of being a rather poorly managed operation. In the same sector, a hundred former *Rangers* joined the *29th US ID,* a substantial reinforcement for the assault waves.

A Ranger in landing uniform. He is equipped with a Bangalore torpedo: a tube filled with explosives intended to open a breach in the barbed wire network. His combat trousers, with its cargo pockets, are much more practical than the standard mustard trousers for carrying equipment
Coll. T. Le Saut

The assault on the Pointe du Hoc has passed into legend. The landslides following the naval bombardments greatly facilitated the Rangers' task. Rope ladders were then duly secured to ensure a less dangerous climb.
Mémorial de Caen

Lieutenant-Colonel De Rudder's command post at the Pointe du Hoc (which can be seen in the background). A Stars and Stripes flag was laid out on top of the cliff to protect themselves from firing from the fleet. The isolated Rangers held out for two days. NARA (© Editions Ouest-France - colorisation Graph&ti)

THE ASSAULT ON THE POINTE DU HOC

The defenders' firing, the soaking ropes and the slippery clay meant that the climb was precarious, but it was made easier by the collapse of the cliff, which had fallen into large heaps after being bombed. At the top, after cleaning up part of the position, the Rangers retrenched and established a block on the coastal road. The Germans, however, maintained strong pressure on the perimeter and isolated bastions, such as the command post, continuing the fight. At 08:30, Sergeants Lommel and Kuhn discovered five pieces of artillery in the vicinity and destroyed them under the noses of dozens of German soldiers. The mission was accomplished.

The insignia of the Rangers. These soldiers were the American equivalent of the British commandos. Coll. T. Le Sant

At the Pointe du Hoc, fighting continued until June 8. The *USS Barton* tried to send a boat to evacuate Rudder's injured men, but a German machine gun put an end to its attempt. Not counting a few paras of the *101st Airborne*, who landed well away from their *Drop Zone*, Rudder finally received, at 21:00, the reinforcement of twenty-three *Rangers* of the *5th*, coming from Omaha. On June 7, thirty other soldiers arrived as reinforcements from the sea, bringing ammunition. They had to wait another two days for the forces landed on *Omaha* to relieve the Rangers. Their losses amounted to 77 killed, 152 wounded and 70 missing.

The rest of the Battle of Normandy was less taxing. The *Rangers* fought towards Grandcamp, then conducted cleaning-up operations and the surveillance of the west coast of the Cotentin Peninsula, after Cherbourg was taken. In September 1944, the *Rangers* were employed during the siege of Brest, the difficult battle of the forest of Hürtgen, and in the Ruhr area before ending the war in Czechoslovakia.

Rudder's Rangers had to remain isolated for two days, reinforced by only a few dozen men. In the centre, Lieutenant Eikner is taking a drink from his canteen. Behind him, a para separated from his 101st ... In the front row on the left, with a bandaged head, Lieutenant-Colonel Trevor: in the Rangers, the officers suffered alongside their men! NARA

352.Infanterie-Division

An Unteroffizier (sergeant) of the 352. ID. The silver braid on his collar marked his status of NCO as well as his individual weapon: the famous MP 40 sub-machine gun. Boots and overalls, model 36, were still worn at this stage of the war. If the division was nothing like an elite unit, it was a solid group which benefited from experienced leadership, including many veterans of the Eastern Front. Coll. T. Le Sant

The *352.ID*, commanded by Generalleutnant Kraiss, was raised in 1943, notably from veterans of the Eastern Front. If the *352.ID* was not an elite unit, however, it was still a good infantry division, totalling 12,734 men, including 7,400 combatants. Three thousand, nine hundred of them were infantrymen, not counting the engineering battalion, unusually strong, and that of reconnaissance (mounted on bicycles). Rommel, aware of the need to reinforce Normandy, dispatched this new unit first to Saint-Lô and then to the Bessin coastline, in February 1944. This movement seemed to go unnoticed by the Allies. The *352.ID* had the advantage of good-quality, new equipment. If many of its soldiers were only young recruits, it also included veterans, and their training was excellent. The anti-tank battalion of the division was particularly well endowed, having ten *Sturmgeschützen*, fourteen *Marder IIIs* and nine *Pak 36s* mounted on *Opel Blitz* lorries; thirty-six 88mm guns in the *Flak-Sturm -Regiment 1*, positioned on the second level close to Nationale 13, could also provide support.

The badge of the 352. ID.

On D-Day, the division conducted a stubborn defence of *Omaha Beach*, inflicting heavy losses on the Americans, and seriously endangering the landing. Through their fighting and their courage, the Americans were finally able to win the battle. The counter-attack against the threatening thrust of the British landing on *Gold Beach* proved to be a total fiasco. A regiment also tried in vain to regain the Pointe du Hoc from Lieutenant-Colonel Rudder's *Rangers*. The *352.ID*, of which we can estimate the losses at 1,200 men on June 6 (200 killed, 500 wounded and 500 missing), therefore failed in its mission.

Its losses were severe, and it could not effectively oppose the enlarging of the bridgehead during the crucial few days which followed D-Day. In three days, Kraiss's division was decimated, but it remained active. On June 9, the *352.ID*, constantly in action since D-Day, had only 2,500 men in the front line, 14 artillery cannons, 16 flak guns and 5 tanks. A huge gap existed over fifteen kilometres

A combat group, photographed at Tilly-sur-Seulles. It is particularly well-armed: three MG 42 machine guns, an MP 40, a semi-automatic rifle. Most of the recruits in the division were, however, inexperienced young conscripts aged just 17 or 18.
Coll. T. Le Sant

Generalleutnant Dietrich Kraiss, commander of the 352. ID. He was 55 years old, and had been decorated with the Iron Cross.
Bundesarchiv

around the forest of Cerisy. Unaware of the weak condition of the German front in the sector held by the disparate remnants of the *352.ID*, the Allies did not manage to take advantage of this opportunity before the arrival of German reinforcements. The *352.ID*, reinforced by part of the *30.Schnelle Brigade* (a mobile brigade), then took up position to the north of Saint-Lô, and participated in the bloody battle of the Hedgerows, making use of a terrain favourable to the defence. By June 24, it had accumulated 5,407 losses. A month later, on the eve of operation *Cobra*, the division was no longer capable of putting more than a *Kampfgruppe* of 650 men into the front line, but its commander also controlled the very experienced remains of four other infantry divisions. Its losses, since June 6, had risen to 8,483 soldiers. Declared out of action by the German High Command on July 30, it was removed from the front in early August, only to be caught up by Patton's leading units, exploiting the breakthrough at Avranches. It could then only fight delaying actions.

The remains of the *352.ID* were integrated into the new *352. Volksgrenadier-Division*, engaged on the southern flank of the Ardennes offensive, in the *VII. Army*. In the spring of 1945, its last units were fighting in Darmstadt, in a *Reich* in ruins.

Utah Beach. One of the German defenders lies beside a casemate. Even though it was supported by the 91.Luftlande-Division, never for a single moment was the 709.ID capable of repulsing the enemy. On the contrary, the 352.ID should not be scorned: fewer than 1,000 men had to face the American onslaught. NARA

THE GERMAN RESISTANCE ON *OMAHA BEACH*

When the astonishing sight of the Allied armada appeared before the eyes of the defenders of *Omaha Becch,* many of the soldiers of *352.* and *716.ID* believed their last hour had come. The German soldiers on *Omaha* had the advantage of formidable defences, albeit unfinished, and a dominant position overlooking the six miles of beach. Eight hundred Germans combatants were to suffer the shock of the American assault. Including reinforcements, Kraiss never had more than 1,500 men to repel the assault waves on *Omaha Beach.* Also engaged at the Pointe du Hoc and on *Gold,* it was to this last sector that Kraiss directed his reserves, due, among other things, to an erroneous report advising him that the situation seemed favourable cn *Omaha.* Despite the German defenders' tenacity and the scale of the losses suffered by the Americans, the *GIs* eventually reduced most of the opposing strongholds. However, despite the bombardment from the naval artillery and the nuisance of the Allied forces, the German reinforcements targeting *Omaha* managed to restrict American progress. The force of Kraiss's counter-attack arrived too late against an enemy which was by then too firmly established to be forced back to sea by the *352 ID* alone.

Utah Beach. One of the German defenders lies beside a casemate. Even though it was supported by the 91.Luftlande-Division, never for a single moment was the 709.ID capable of repulsing the enemy. On the contrary, the 352.ID should not be scorned: fewer than 1,000 men had to face the American onslaught. NARA

These Marder IIIs, photographed at Roncey, had been rendered *hors de combat.* Their fragile look was an illusion: their formidable 75 mm Pak 40 guns were capable of overcoming any Allied armoured car up to 2,000 m away. The 352. ID had 14 of them. NARA

716.Infanterie-Division

This unit, raised in May 1941, was commanded by Generalleutnant Richter. As with the other units securing the defence of the Atlantic Wall, the *716.ID* had to transfer a portion of its strength to the Eastern Front and, being designed from the start as a division of occupation, had many older soldiers in its ranks, including the sick and convalescent. From 17,000 men in 1943, it had decreased to 7,771 men by May 1st 1944. That seemed very few to fulfill its mission, which was to secure the coastal defences between the estuaries of the Orne and the Vire. The units were therefore spread out on various points along the coast. However, stationed in the region of Caen since June 1942, the division had a significant advantage, since it knew every inch of the defence sector to which it was allocated. Moreover, the arrival of the *352.ID*, in February, had relieved Richter's left flank to an extent, although some of his units still remained in what was to become *Omaha Beach*. The sector allocated to the *716.ID* also included the army and navy coastal batteries,

A German infantryman, typical of summer 1944: the 716 was made up of such men. ID: K 98 rifle, steel helmet model 42 with raw edges, smock model 42, boots and gaiters. He is a veteran: he boasts the ribbon of the Iron Cross, Second Class, as well as the insignia of the assault infantry. Coll. T. Le Sant

Canadian motorcyclists, perhaps from the Military Police, are starting to search their prisoners. These men belong to the 5th Company of Grenadier Regiment 736 of 716.ID. The division was all but wiped out; for them, the war was over. IWM

especially at Longues, the Pointe du Hoc, Mont Fleury and Ouistreham. To expand his meagre resources, Richter was able to add three battalions of *Osttruppen*. The division also had an independent anti-tank unit, with 10 heavy self-propelled anti-tank vehicles, 11 *Pak 40* and *Pak 43/41*s and 2 self-propelled 2 cm *Flak Cannon*s.

To repulse the invasion, the 716. ID could rely on the fortifications and its many anti-tank guns, like this 50 mm in its bunker near Pegasus Bridge.
Photo T. Le Sant

THE TENACIOUS DEFENCE OF *THE HILLMAN STRONGHOLD*

The resistance offered by *WN 17 - Hillman's* code name for the Allies - was one of the highlights of D-Day. Far from surrendering quickly to the assailants, the German soldiers of the *Grenadier-Regiment 736* at Oberst Ludwig's HQ resisted. Towards 15:00, the machine guns of the *WN 17* mowed down one hundred and sixty Tommies of the *1st Norfolk,* who had recklessly pressed too close to the German position during their advance toward the interior. The attackers of the *1st Suffolk,* whose mission was to neutralise *Hillman,* first had to clear passages through the belt of barbed wire and try to neutralise the GFM cloches and the anti-tank vehicles of the position. In spite of the courage of the *1st Suffolk,* the intervention of armoured personnel carriers from the *18th Hussars* and *Sherman Flails* was necessary, and it was only towards 22:00 that the British penetrated into the position. The various delays by the *8th Brigade* and the rest of the *3rd Division* proved detrimental in the planned operation in the direction of Caen.

On June 6, 1944, the *716.ID* was bearing the full brunt of the Allied armada's assault on the beaches of *Omaha, Gold, Juno* and *Sword.* The main unit to oppose the onslaught of the Allied power on that fateful day, the division could not hope to defeat the enemy on its own. Despite its tenacity, the division's positions fell one after another. The best successes were obtained on *Omaha,* with the *352.ID,* and on *Juno,* faced with the Canadians confronting a tenacious opponent, where they did not hesitate to take advantage of the many tunnels connecting their own positions to open fire on the assailant from the rear, from a sector assumed to be secure. On *Gold,* on the other hand, the resistance held out, despite the severe losses inflicted on the English from the Hamel stronghold. On *Sword,* in spite of the belated support of the *21.Panzer,* the *716.ID* could not prevent the landed forces joining up with the airborne troops. On the other hand, the road to Caen was blocked. The fact was that Richter lost approximately 3,000 men on June 6 (860 killed, 560 wounded and 1,270 missing): almost half of his force.

Having lost all combat capacity, the division had to be removed from the front on June 15 to regroup in the south of France. However, some of its units - around 1,700 men and half of the *Osttruppen* - remained attached to other divisions, and the departure of Richter's division only took effect in the first half of July. The losses in Normandy were estimated at 6,300 men.

These Fallschirmjäger represented the elite of the German Wehrmacht, while the 716. ID, the static division, on the contrary, was the same type of unit in the second order. However, Richter's soldiers fought valiantly, one against ten.
Bundesarchiv

21.Panzerdivision

The 21. Panzer-Division included many veterans of Africa and Russia in its ranks. It was a strong unit. In 1944, many Panzergrenadiere wore a camouflage smock and a helmet-cover on their Stahlhelme.
Coll. T. Le Sant

The training of the *21.Panzerdivision* cannot be compared to that of the other armoured divisions. Raised in Africa in 1941 from the *5. Leichte-Division* and a regiment of the *15.Panzerdivision,* together with the latter it formed the famous *Afrikakorps*. Destroyed in Tunisia in 1943, a new *21.Panzer* was raised during the summer of 1943, from the *Schnelle Brigade West*. The quality of recruits was very variable, since the unit, made up of 16,925 men on June 1 1944, included as many of the surplus from other units as soldiers newly mobilized in Germany, plus 2,000 veterans of the *Afrikakorps*. At that time, in addition to a few outdated French machines, the division, commanded by Generalleutnant Feuchtinger, had 98 long-barrelled *Panzer IVs*, six short-barrelled *Panzer IVs* and six former *Panzer IIIs*, now dedicated to command functions. The striking force of the division was strengthened by the presence of armoured cars on French, and sometimes German, chassis, 120 in total. Many of these vehicles were armed with the formidable *Pak 40* or 105mm guns. In addition, a far from negligible asset, its anti-tank battalion comprised twenty-four 88mm *Pak*. The artillery was also large, especially including *Nebelwerfer,* so that the division, far from being second rate, represented a formidable foe.

Insignia of the 21.Panzerdivision

THE BELATED COUNTER-ATTACK ON *SWORD BEACH*

The absence of Rommel in Germany, and of Feuchtinger, with his mistress in Paris, as well as the slow speed with which the German High Command authorised the engagement, goes a long way towards explaining the failure of the *21.Panzer* on June 6. Confusion marked this decisive day. When Feuchtinger joined his HQ, then that of the *716.ID,* he had no telephone contact with its units; he could only communicate by sending messengers, because he had not brought a radio! A mass attack of the *21.Panzer* against the *6th Airborne*'s bridgehead, still very precarious, could have met with success. Moreover, had they faced the firing of the Allied armada, an early intervention in the Anglo-Canadian landings would have drastically affected progress - already limited since *Sword Beach* - with all the consequences that this would have had on the consolidation of the bridgehead. The about-turn imposed on the *Panzer* in the middle of the morning, while they were en route to confront the airborne troops, caused considerable delays. The counter-attack towards the coast only took place at the end of afternoon, and held out. Nevertheless, the Germans reached the shoreline at Luc-sur-Mer, where they were met with the unforgettable sight of the Allied armada. On the evening of June 6, access was still being maintained between the beaches of *Juno* and *Sword.*

Major Becker, whose workshop produced powerful self-propelled guns for the division, Generalleutnant Feuchtinger, who was with his mistress in Paris on the night of June 6, and Generalfeldmarshall Rommel, also absent when the invasion began. Bundesarchiv

Its training was supervised by Geyr von Schweppenburg, the leader of the *Panzergruppe West* in person. However, the preparations to repel the invasion - such as the establishment of 'Rommel's asparagus' - as well as the frantic pace of successive reallocations of the division between June 1943 and June 1944, before being finally stationed in the Caen region, was detrimental to their preparation for combat. The only *Panzer* division at the front on D-Day, the *21.Panzer* did not push the Allies back to the sea. However Feuchtinger, aware of the crucial importance of Caen, managed to deny them access.

This Marder III was long considered as a machine belonging to the 21.Panzer, who never had armoured vehicles of this type; in fact it belonged to an infantry division in opposition to American paratroops, believed to be the 243.ID, or even the 346.ID or the 716.ID, all of which operated in the 6th Airborne's sector. The wing hanging from the hedge indicates the wreckage of a Horsa. Bundesarchiv.

Panzergrenadiere of the 21.Panzer are escorting their prisoners, of the 6th Airborne. Camouflage uniforms were used more and more in the course of the Second World War, although they were more common in the German formations. The 21.Panzer, an elite unit, had missed the opportunity to wipe out the British paras on D-Day. **Bundesarchiv.**

For the last time, Rommel inspects the 21. Panzer-Division in May 1944. He was reviewing self-propelled guns on French chassis. Far from being inefficient machines, these guns provided anti-tank support and very important artillery.
Bundesarchiv

An officer of the 21. Panzer in camouflage uniform in the Troarn sector. Although not equipped with Panthers, the 21. Panzer-Division was powerful and proved to be capable of blocking access to Caen for over a month.
Coll. T. Le Sant

The *21.Panzer* then confronted the British for two months to the north and west of the city, offering a stubborn resistance which bore witness to its value. But 2,597 men were lost on June 16. On July 3, a report stated that the *21.Panzer* had destroyed 101 Allied tanks since June 6. According to Rommel himself, it was the British artillery which stopped any attempt to counter-attack on July 8 and 9. That day, the *21.Panzer* had to abandon the left bank of Caen to an enemy which it had forced to pay dearly for liberation. *Operation Goodwood* hit the powerful Kampfgruppe head on, and caused significant losses to the division. Nevertheless, the *Sturmgeschützen* played an essential role in the failure of the breakthrough desired by Monty. The losses amounted to 4,307 men by July 31. The division then left the front at Caen, to oppose *Operation Bluecoat*, without success. It came out of the cauldron of Falaise considerably weakened; its losses totalled 8,000 men. In the meantime, nearly 2,500 replacements had been integrated into the division to fill some of these losses. It was therefore a weakened division which escaped from the Falaise Pocket before crossing the river Seine.

The *21.Panzer* was re-formed in the autumn of 1944 and fought in Lorraine, then, at the beginning of 1945, took part in the *Nordwind* counter-offensive in Alsace. Transferred to the East, it met the Red Army for the first time, before which it had to lay down its arms at the end of the war.

Number of operational *Panzer* and *Panzerjäger*

June 1	150
July 17	50[1]
August 6	20[1]
August 22	10[1]

1 : Number of the only *Panzer*

Fallschirmjäger-Regiment 6

A Fallschirmjäger, grenade in hand. He is wearing the famous para helmet, the camouflage smock typical of his unit, and jump boots. He has made himself a non-regulation scarf.
Coll. T. Le Sant

This regiment of the *2. Fallschirmjäger-Division* was sent to the Cotentin Peninsula in May 1944, constituting a welcome reinforcement to assist the *91.Luftlande-Division*, to which it was tactically linked for its supplies. It was commanded by Major von der Heydte, very satisfied with his *Fallschirmjäger*, whose average age was seventeen-and-a-half. The unit was particularly well equipped with collective weapons, since each combat group had two machine guns instead of one. In addition, the regiment was very well equipped with communications equipment. On the other hand, its *Pak* guns were not available until after the Landings. Von der Heydte rectified this inadequacy by imposing rigorous training on the handling of portable anti-tank weapons and mines. At the beginning of June 1944, its strength had reached 3,457 men, 1,000 other combatants being received as reinforcements during the month.

Insignia of the Fallschirmjäger-Regiment 6

The Jabos, Allied fighter bombers, were a threat at all times. The camouflage paint and the branches arranged over the vehicle were not enough: three men were scanning the skies. The Falschirmjäger standing on the bonnet is a Feldgendarme, recognisable by the high collar which earned them the nickname of 'guard dogs'. Bundesarchiv.

CARENTAN

On June 9, the *Fallschirmjäger* were pushed south of the Douve. After being reorganized, the *101st Airborne* launched into the assault on Carentan. A little prematurely, Major-General Maxwell Taylor invited the *FJR 6* to surrender. In response, the guns of the *4./ Artillerie-Regiment 91,* supporting the *Fallschirmjäger,* fired their last explosive shells. The US paratroopers, however, had the advantage of numbers. The *Fallschirmjäger* soon found themselves short of ammunition, and suffered heavy casualties. In the night of June 10 - 11, the Luftwaffe dropped thirteen tonnes of supplies, but this proved inadequate. Threatened by the *327th Glider Regiment* on his left flank, Heydte decided to withdraw his troops and to abandon the town to the Americans. A rear-guard ensured the safety of the manoeuvre until dawn on June 12. The 'Lions of Carentan', to use von Choltitz's expression, had been unable to oppose the American pressure: to Rommel's dismay, the *Omaha* and *Utah* bridgeheads were united from then on.

A group of tank destroyers take shelter behind a wall. An ambush was especially dangerous when faced with a steel monster: handling a Panzerschreck, the German equivalent of the bazooka, was no sinecure. Coll. P. Tiquet

The *FJR 6* was integrated into a plan against a possible airborne attack. Rommel and Meindl, the leader of the *2.Fallschirmkorps,* forced a reluctant von der Heydte to establish several defensive positions between Carentan, Periers and Mont Castre. The lack of means of locomotion - seventy vehicles in fifty different models! - combined with the sabotage carried out by the Resistance, weighed heavily on the possibilities of reaction by German paratroopers on D-Day. Under these conditions, no coordinated counter-attack was possible.

The losses, on the contrary, were very heavy for those German paratroopers, since a battalion was completely destroyed by the *101st Airborne,* on June 7. Engaged in a marshy area without being able to take cover, 350 paras of the 1st battalion were captured and 150 killed or seriously injured. Twenty-five men were only just able to reach the German lines. But Rommel sorely lacked the means to resist across the entire front of the invasion. Von der Heydte had to provide the bulk of the defence against the American advance south from the *Utah Beach* bridgehead. On the evening of June 11, the *FJR 6* was forced to abandon the important Carentan crossroads to the Americans.

The terrible Hedgerow War ensued. By early July, the unit, tested but still operational, was pushed back towards Periers. By July 14, the regiment had no more than 20% of its theoretical heavy weapon equipment left. After the success of *Operation Cobra,* launched on July 25, the regiment was decimated in the Roncey pocket. A significantly decreased *Kampfgruppe* still stood on the front line, but only for a short time. On August 10, the remains of the regiment - which did not amount to more than about sixty fighting men - had to be removed from the Normandy front to be reorganised in Nancy. The last fighting took place in the Tinchebray sector. There were no more than 1,007 men left, out of the 4,500 who had fought in Normandy with the regiment. The unit was re-formed, and fought in Holland from September 1944 onwards.

The Fallschirmjäger had captured a jeep. It was a Godsend: they were desperately short of vehicles. The FJR 6 had 70, in 50 different models. In the background, in the farm garage, can be seen a Schwimmwagen, that is, an amphibious Volkswagen. Coll. P. Tiquet

Putting an MG 42 on a heavy carriage into a battery, in an artfully camouflaged firing position. The Fallschirmjäger units received a double issue of machine guns.
Coll. P. Tiquet

One of the 3,000 Püppchen 88 mm Raketenwerfer 43 antitank guns produced for the Wehrmacht. The rocket is the same as that of the Panzerschreck, but the gun was more accurate and more stable. Not bulky, it was an ideal weapon for the paratroops.
Photo T. Le Sant

12.SS Panzerdivision « Hitlerjügend »

A machine- gunner of the Hitlerjugend. The Waffen SS were distinguished by wearing camouflage uniforms with different designs from those of the Wehrmacht. In position in the fields of ripe wheat, this soldier has fixed ears of corn to the straps of his reversible helmet-cover. In his left hand, he is carrying a drum magazine for his MG 42.
Coll. T. Le Sant

On June 6 1944, the *12.SS Panzer,* raised in 1943 from members of the Hitler Youth, was controlled by SS-Brigadeführer Witt. It amounted to 20,540 men. Their effectiveness, however, was lacking because fewer than half of the total strength had been trained: a significant stumbling block. The division, nevertheless, constituted a formidable unit. On June 1, Witt commanded 97 *Panzer IVs* and 66 *Panthers,* a total of 163 armoured personnel carriers. Twenty-one *Jagdpanzer IVs* were used within the unit, but did not reach the front before the month of July. Fifty-nine *Panzers* were sent in replacement between June and September. The artillery equipment was complete, and the *Panzergrenadiere* regiments had over 306 operational half-tracks, giving them an all-terrain mobility close to that of tanks. These regiments were particularly well equipped with anti-tank weapons, since 24 *Pak 40s* were available. Witt could also count on twelve 88mm *Flak* guns. From April 1944 onwards, the *Hitlerjügend* was mainly confined to the Eure region.

On June 6, before

The Hitlerjugend's emblem : a rune crossed with a key, underlining the link with the 1.SS 'Liebstandarte Adolf Hitler', which had supplied some of their officers.

BURON

On June 7, the *Hitlerjügend* received the order to counter-attack toward the coast, in concert with the *21.Panzer*. Towards 13:00, observing the advance of units of the *3rd Canadian Division* from his command post at the abbey of Ardenne, Kurt Meyer, leader of the *25.SS Panzergrenadier-Regiment,* decided to seize the opportunity to strike at the flank of a careless opponent. The *Waffen SS* ambush stopped the progress of the *North Nova Scotia Highlanders* to Authie in its tracks. Forced back beyond Buron, the Canadians were able, however, to stop the *SS* momentum. Three hundred and five Canadian soldiers and many tanks were lost, including 28 of the *Sherbrooke Fusiliers*. The *Hitlerjügend* suffered significant losses: 6 *Panzer IVs* and 386 men. More seriously, the counter-attack designed to push the Allies back to the sea took a long time. On that same June 7 and 8, twenty-seven unfortunate Canadians, captured at Authie and Buron, were executed by firing squad in the gardens of Ardenne abbey of Ardenne. This crime was not the last committed by the *SS* in Normandy.

The 12.SS Panzer-Division 'Hitlerjungend' comprised many young soldiers aged from barely 16 to 18. Fanatical, well equipped and supplied with good-quality weapons, they were redoubtable fighters. This Waffen SS soldier is remarkably well camouflaged: his face is blackened and he has added leaves to his helmet. He is also wearing a jacket camouflaged in several shades, particularly well planned. Bundesarchiv.

receiving the order but acting on the basis of the reports which had reached him, Witt took the initiative to put his division on alert at 03:00. Some reconnaissance units progressed to the coast on June 6, but the order to march towards Caen was only given at 17:00. The reconnaissance unit went ahead of the division, and the advance party reached the coast, where the strength of the Anglo-Saxon coalition was revealed to the *Waffen SS.*

The SS advance in line, the last with a Panzerfaust on his shoulder. The Hitlerjugend fought fanatically outside Caen, not hesitating to assassinate its prisoners in cold blood, on several occasions. Archives du Calvados

This member of the SS had clearly been badly beaten at the time of his capture. Hatred had arisen between the Canadians and the Waffen SS since the latter had put prisoners to death. PAC

Brigade Major Kingsmill told a war correspondent about the fanaticism of the *Waffen SS*: "Our men witnessed the senseless slaughter of the Hitler Youth. [...] over there here, another young man shot himself in the mouth. The P. 38 is still there! Major Wilson [...] saw the lad commit suicide while he was about to take him prisoner."

One thousand, four hundred and seventeen men were lost by the *Hitlerjügend* between June 6 -16. Witt, killed on June 14, was replaced by Kurt Meyer, known as 'Panzermeyer'. By July 9, their losses had reached perhaps 5,400 men. Forty-one *Panzers* had been permanently destroyed up to June 26, the total reaching ninety-three on July 9, the date on which the left bank of Caen is cleared.

From June 7 onwards, the *Hitlerjügend* launched a counter-attack, meeting the Canadian's progress head on and inflicting significant losses. The following night, the first *Panther* destroyed during the Battle of Normandy belonged to the *Hitlerjügend,* and was probably the result of friendly fire. These *Panzers,* regarded as the best armoured vehicles of the conflict, suffered heavy losses on June 9, when seven *Panthers* were destroyed by fire in the space of four minutes. Did the *Hitlerjügend* have too few experienced recruits? Entrenched on a front line stretching over fifteen kilometres, it was one of the pillars of the defence of the capital of Lower Normandy. The legend of the *Hitlerjügend* was born of the ferocity of the fighting. On July 9,

On July18, the division was at rest, with the possibility of being moved toward the Bay of Somme, where the real Landings could have taken place. But the launch of *Operation Goodwood* forced von Kluge to make the *Hitlerjügend* intervene again, south of Caen . The *12.SS Panzer* took part in the violent

Units of the12. SS Panzer-Division in the course of *Operation Charnwood.* This time, they had to abandon the left bank at Caen to the Allies. Archives du Calvados

fighting in August on the Caen - Falaise axis, offering a particularly relentless resistance in Falaise, although the image of the defence to the death of the girls' school was forged after the war, and actually took place in Épinal. Their losses in the Normandy Campaign were estimated at 8,000 men.

The division, which managed to cross the Seine, was re-formed to fight in the Ardennes counter-offensive in December 1944, in the course of which it did not perform particularly well, contradicting its reputation of being an elite unit. Its ultimate offensive, to Budapest in 1945, was also a resounding failure.

Number of operational *Panzer* and *Panzerjäger*

June 1	139
July 6	60
August 6	56
August 21	10

SS of the Hitlerjugend on the front page of the propaganda! This photograph, taken at La Villeneuve-de-Rots on June 9 1944, shows a machine-gunner dressed in overalls made out of Italian tent canvas. He has a spare gun on his back and several rounds of ammunition round his neck and in his ammunition pouch.
Bundesarchiv

Panzer Lehr-Division

A tank crew member of the Panzer Lehr wearing the Panzerschütze black uniform with the death's-head, the insignia of the armoured troops, and the pink braid of the armoured units on his collar tabs and shoulders. Coll. T. Le Sant

The *Panzer Lehr*, 14,699 soldiers strong, was beyond a doubt the *Wehrmacht's* best equipped armoured division. Commanded by Generalleutnant Bayerlein, it was formed at the beginning of 1944 from different training units for the specific purpose of opposing the expected Allied invasion. It was, therefore, an elite group, which was clearly shown by its issue of equipment. Apart from 19 *Panzer*s, collected in replacements during the battle, the *Panzer Lehr* actually possessed 234 armoured personnel carriers: five *Tiger IIs* (not engaged in Normandy), 89 *Panthers*, 99 *Panzer IVs*, 10 *Sturmgeschützen* and 31 *Jagdpanzer IVs*. Most unusually, the four battalions of *Panzergrenadiere* were fully equipped with half-tracked vehicles, and each had 39 *Panzerschreck* , eight 75 mm guns and nine 37mm guns mounted on half-tracks. The *Flak* battalion was equally well equipped with eighteen 88mm guns instead of the eight or twelve generally issued to other units. Ensuring the essential fire support, the artillery canon were usually self-propelled. In addition, like the *2.Panzer*, the reconnaissance battalion had a rare and particularly sophisticated device: the *Puma*.

Insignia of the Panzer Lehr-Division

The *bocage*: deep, winding paths, ideal for ambush, where it was often difficult to move in a tank with gun barrel as long as this Panther's, of the Panzer Lehr. The Panzergrenadieres on the right, wearing double-breasted jackets, were essential to ensure the Panzer's safety. Archives du Calvados

The Panther battalion of the Panzer Lehr Panther had been seconded to them by the 3. Panzer-Division. On June 6, the powerful tanks were en route to Russia: the trains had to be stopped to recall them! BnF

Active in March 1944 in Hungary, when Hitler had feared a breakdown of their alliance, the *Panzer Lehr* was deployed in the Le Mans sector in May 1944. In spite of the threat of imminent invasion, the *Panther* battalion, which actually belonged to the *3.Panzerdivision*, was loaded on trains to Poland. The announcement of the Landings caused an immediate counter-order. Yet it was not until late in the afternoon of June 6 that the *Panzer Lehr* finally set off for the Normandy coast. The five columns of the unit were therefore moving in broad daylight. Initial losses were recorded, but the holdups imposed by the attacks of *Jabos* caused much more serious consequences . On June 9, Rommel ordered Bayerlein to re-take Bayeux, which had fallen on June 7, because the small town controlled the N 13. This axis of strategic communication formed a bypass parallel to the Front, essential to ensure the consistency of the defence between the Cotentin and Caen. But the enemy could not be pushed back to the sea straight away. A war of positions followed in the Tilly-sur-Seulles sector, where the fights were very hard-won.

THE BATTLE OF LINGÈVRES

After the failure of the counter-attack on Bayeux on June 8, the *Panzer Lehr* was deployed against the *30th British Corps* whose progress towards Tilly-sur-Seulles was slowed down. On June 14, after several days of particularly hard-fought clashes, the *9th Durham Light Infantry* of the *50th ID* finally managed to liberate Lingèvres. Bayerlein responded promptly but the fighting was turning to the advantage of the British. A *Sherman Firefly* succeeded in destroying five *Panthers*. The *Panzer Lehr* still remained in the area of Tilly-sur-Seulles for almost a month . This counter-employment of a division of *Panzers* forced Bayerlein to retire his half-tracked troop transports from the front line, temporarily useless, while the losses within the regiments of *Panzergrenadiere* never ceased to rise. Two thousand, nine hundred and seventy-two men and fifty *Panzers* were lost in June.

This impressive view of a Panther of the Panzer Lehr clearly shows the slope of the armour-plating of the 'beast', which added to the way it deflected incoming shells, and the thickness of the steel to be pierced. Side skirts protected the tracks and their bearers against light weapon fire. This tank, vastly superior to the Sherman, did not, however, enter the battle before the evening of June 8 ... DR

This impressive view of a Tiger I of the Schwere SS Panzer-Abteilung 101 perfectly illustrates the feeling of power which emanated from these Panzers. It's easy to imagine the genuine awe felt by the Allied soldiers suddenly coming face to face with such a monster. Behind it, barely visible, is a second Tiger being towed by this one. Bundesarchiv.

By July 3, a report established its score at 154 Allied tanks destroyed.

On July 10, the *Panzer Lehr*, relieved by the *272.ID*, was transferred to oppose the Americans. It launched a counter-attack towards Le Dézert, on a field highly unsuitable for the deployment of *Panzers*. After a promising beginning, the tenacity of the *GIs* of the *9th* and the *30th US ID* and the combined action of the *Tank Destroyers* and the *Jabos*, got the better of *Kampfgruppen* Welsch and Scholze, who were forced to abandon the few pieces of terrain they had gained after having suffered heavy losses.

After this setback, the *Panzer Lehr* went on the defensive to the north-west of Saint-Lô, with reserves established around Percy. It was on these positions that it was hit hard by *Cobra's* carpet bombing: Bayerlein claimed to have lost 2,150 soldiers on July 24 and 25, including the troops attached to the *Panzer Lehr.* Undeniably, the defence, which lacked reserves and depth, was disorganised, and the effect on the morale of the combatants was sure. Hoping for the intervention of the reserves, the

The Panzer Lehr had enough half-track SPWs for all its Panzergrenadiere but, in the *bocage*, they were of little use. Bundesarchiv. (© Editions Ouest-France - colorisation Graph&ti)

Panzergrenadiere and a few *Panzers* offered a stubborn resistance on the first day of the offensive, but the unit collapsed and could not play a role of any significance until the end of the campaign. The losses of artillery pieces were high, and several *Panzers* under repair had had to be abandoned to an enemy advancing at speed.

While a small detachment, von Hausser's *Kampfgruppe* remained at the Front until August 12, most of the *Panzer Lehr* was evacuated towards Alençon, then Fontainebleau. Only the Kuhnow *Kampfgruppe* remained, locked in the Falaise Cauldron, but it managed to escape on August 20. The losses in Normandy reached a total of 7,411 men, but 3,437 replacements and convalescent patients joined the unit in June and July.

Re-equipped without reaching its *Panzer* strength of June 1944, the *Panzer Lehr* was engaged in the Battle of the Bulge, in the Bastogne sector. It then took part in the fighting for the defence of the Reich and disappeared in the Ruhr Pocket in April 1945.

A Type D Panther, like those of the I/Pz Rgt 6. This machine, perfectly preserved, was nevertheless decorated with the most fantastic markings. Coll. T. Le Sant

Number of operational *Panzer* and *Panzerjäger*

June 1	223
July 1	96
August 1	33
August 22	20

7th British Armoured Division « Desert Rats »

Every armoured division had its own infantry escort, but cooperation with the armoured cars frequently left something to be desired. This infantryman from the 7th Armoured carries extra pouches for Bren magazines.
Coll. T. Le Sant

This man wears a uniform specific to tank crews, whereas others preferred to retain their battle-dress. The man is wearing a throat microphone and headphones. He has stuck his leather gloves into his belt. Glasses were useful when dust and smoke enveloped the battlefield.
Coll. T. Le Sant

Units of the 7th Armoured Division land in Normandy on D-Day + 1: here, a Cromwell tank. Much to their annoyance, the 'Desert Rats' of the 22nd Armoured Brigade had had to give up their Shermans, except the Firefly, fitted with a powerful 17-pound gun, to be re- equipped with this tank, which was hardly a success, and which was also used by the division's reconnaissance regiment, the 8th King's Royal Irish Hussars. IWM

Created in Egypt in 1938 as a mobile division, then organised as an armoured division, Major-General Erskine's *7th Armoured Division* was an experienced unit, as was illustrated during the Desert War, before they were engaged in Sicily and then Italy. Transferred to Great Britain in view of *Operation Overlord*, the division had in its ranks many veterans of North Africa who believed they had done their part in this war.

After the first units landed on June 7, their first battles consisted of the reduction of pockets, such as that of Port-en-Bessin, before taking part in the battle of Tilly-sur-Seulles. The *Desert Rats* were confused by the wooded Normandy landscape, and the setback at Villers-Bocage on June,13, so soon after D-Day, shook their confidence. The division therefore remained on the defensive until June 30, then had a three-week rest period. Their losses amounted to 1,149 men.

The *Desert Rats* returned to action with *Operation Goodwood,* but the hold-ups and the unit's lack of enthusiasm for combat meant that its participation in this massive attack of armoured cars turned into a fiasco. Nevertheless, on July 20, the division's tank crews did not lack courage in their commitment towards the crest of Bourguébus. The offensive cost less than thirty tanks. The *7th Armoured Division* then provided valuable support to the Canadians during *Operation Spring* . Twenty-one tanks were lost. Shortly after, the division was once again involved in a major operation, in this case *Operation Bluecoat*. The final objective, Aunay-sur-Odon, however, was not reached. Montgomery, who, most unfairly, was seeking whom to blame for the failure, relieved Erskine of his command and entrusted the division to Major-General Lloyd-Verney. Many of the soldiers were tired of war, and cases of desertion were multiplying.

A British armoured division had thousands of machines, which were not easy to deploy. This soldier and the vehicles which surround him, however, had little to fear from the Luftwaffe. Coll. T. Le Sant

The famous jerboa, adopted in Egypt as the divisional emblem during the Desert War. Coll. T. Le Sant

Captain Cotton and his crew take a break in front of their tank, a Cromwell IV armed with a 95 mm gun, intended not for the anti-tank battle but for support. These men belong to the 4th County of London Yeomanry, which was decimated by the Tigers at Villers-Bocage. Cotton, seen on the left with his looted Iron Cross, earned his promotion by the end of this action. Note the cartoon character decorating the bodywork of the tank, on the machine-gun side at the front. IWM

On June 13, the 'Desert Rats' of the 1st Bn (Motor), The Rifle Brigade examine the personal effects of their prisoners, who had probably belonged to the Panzer Lehr. The two Germans on the left are former Gebirgsjäger (Alpine troops) from which they had kept - on the right-the emblem: an edelweiss. The guards are very lightly armed: it certainly cannot have been them who had effected the capture. IWM

VILLERS-BOCAGE

On June 13, the division started a daring encircling manoeuvre in the context of *Operation Perch*. The German front was seriously threatened, and the *Panzer Lehr* prey to great danger. A British column, formed of the *22nd Armoured Brigade* and support units, went up the N 175. However, the *7th Arm. Div.* showed a lack of speed, and came to a complete standstill following the famous intervention of Wittman's *Tiger*, which surprised the halted column. The *Panzers* sowed chaos: ten tanks and nearly thirty British armoured cars were destroyed. The *Panzer IV* of the *Panzer Lehr* and other *Tiger I* took part in the skirmish, but fighting in an urban environment without infantry support is a mistake. Thirty British tanks were destroyed: the defeat of the *7th Arm. Div.* was indisputable. The British advance was stopped dead.

The *7th Armoured Division* then took part in actions of secondary importance in the reduction of the Falaise Pocket. The fighting in the area around Mont Pinçon as well as the advance towards Conde-sur-Noireau, were the scene of a bitter, costly struggle, due to the topography of la Suisse Normande ('Norman Switzerland').

An American M3 half-track. This vehicle was used by the motorised infantry battalions of the British Armoured Divisions. Coll. T. Le Sant

Armoured vehicles from the 7th Armoured Division (4th County of London Yeomanry) land at Ver-sur-Mer in the sunshine of June 7. The machines are still fitted with their waterproofing systems. IWM

On August 10, after the loss of a thousand men in three consecutive weeks at *Goodwood*, the major part of the unit was removed from the front. The *7th Arm. Div.* then took part in the pursuit of the enemy, which was no longer conducting anything more than delaying actions, although these were not without success. Saint-Pierre-sur-Dives was reached on August 16 but, on the Lisieux road, hard fighting still awaited the *Desert Rats*, faced with the *Kampfgruppen* enemy. At the end of August, the armoured regiment lacked a third of its tanks, and 50% of its strength within the infantry brigade of the *7th Arm. Div.*

After a drive through the north of France on the heels of the retreating *Wehrmacht*, the 7th *Arm. Div.* fought in Belgium and then in Holland. At the end of April 1945, it reached Hamburg.

A column of the 7th Armoured Division in the Mont Pinçon sector. The division showed a lack of enthusiasm during *Operation Bluecoat*, following which its commander, Erskine, was dismissed. IWM

Les Tiger des Schweres Panzer-Abteilungen 101.SS, 102.SS et 503

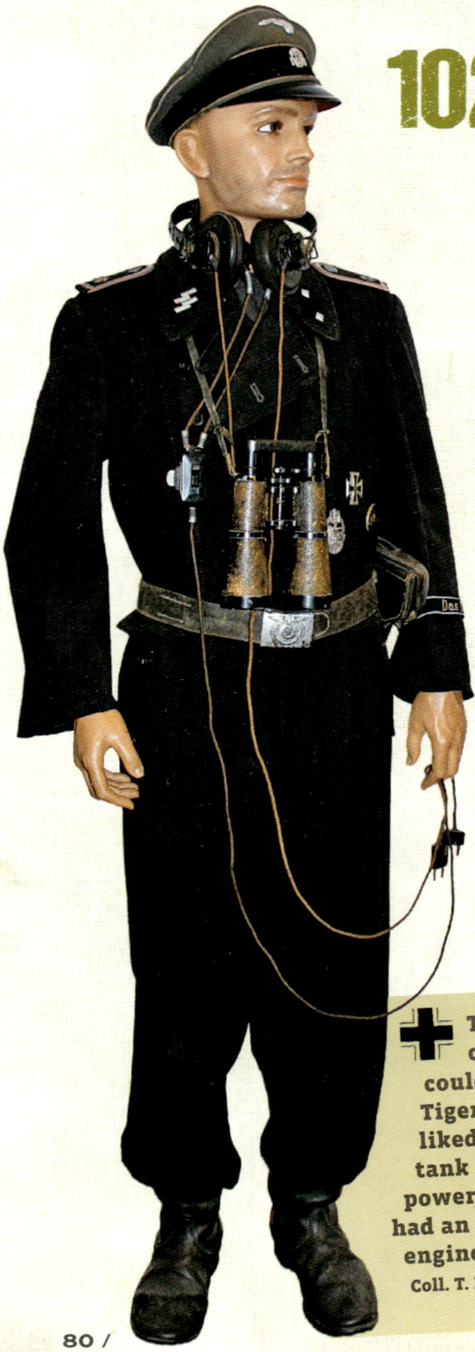

This SS Panzer commander could command a Tiger, a machine liked by German tank crews for its power, but which had an unreliable engine.
Coll. T. Le Sant

Three battalions of the heavy tanks *Tiger I and Tiger II*, the *'Königstiger'*, took part in the Battle of Normandy. Each battalion had 45 *Tigers*. The *101.Schweres SS Panzer-Abteilung,* commanded by SS-Sturmbahnführer von Westernhagen, was stationed in the region of Gournay-en-Bray. On June 6, 1944, SS-Obersturmbahnführer's *102.Schweres SS Panzer-Abteilung* was stationed in the Netherlands, and had not yet received all its *Tigers*. Hauptmann Fromme's *503.Schweres Panzer-Abteilung*, the only *Panzer* to have *Königstiger* (to the number of twelve), was still in Germany when the Landings took place.

Under the constant threat of the Allied aviators, getting them to the Front Line was carried out by train or road. In this particular case, the journey, in stages, was carried out by night when possible. The distance to travel was not without effect on the fragile mechanics of the engines, and the tracks were put under severe strain. The first battalion ready for action in Normandy was the *101. Schweres SS Panzer-Abteilung*. Arriving on June 12, the first *Tiger* made a thunderous entry into battle by carrying out an explosive action in Villers-Bocage. German propaganda seized on this feat of arms by Michael Wittmann, then the company commander. Taking advantage of the hedgerows and the Tiger's fire power, Wittmann and his men set fire to some thirty tanks and dozens of armoured vehicles. Nevertheless, three *Tigers* were destroyed in the street fighting which ensued. During the night of June 14 -15, an air raid near Évrecy destroyed four other *Tigers*. By July 5, the battalion's losses already amounted to fifteen, or one-third of its initial strength.

Michael Wittmann's escapade with his Tiger at Villers-Bocage was well known. However, the final cost for the Germans was very heavy: six Tigers were destroyed that day ... Caen Memorial

Insignia of the Schwere Panzer-Abteilungen 101.SS

Westernhagen's *Tigers* were no longer alone. On July 1, Weiss's 45 *Tigers*, then quartered in the park of the Château of Versailles after having been repositioned from the Pas-de-Calais, took the road to the Front. The battalion went into action on July 9 in the Hill 112 sector, where the *101.s SS-Pz-Abt.* were also fighting. Despite the bitterness of the combat, by July 31 Weiss had only lost 3 *Tigers*.

CHÊNEDOLLÉ

The fighting at Chênedollé illustrated the legend which surrounded the heavy *Tiger* tank. At the beginning of August 22, the *102.s SS-Pz-Abt.* was fighting at the side of the *Hohenstaufen* and the *3.Fallschirmjäger-Divisions* in the Vire-Estry-Chênedollé sector, particularly in the area of Hill 119. The *bocage* did not make the deployment of *Tigers* easy. However, on August 3, SS-Ustuf Loritz destroyed six enemy tanks, two other armoured vehicles being burned by SS-Hscha Treng's *Tiger*, bringing the score in armoured vehicles destroyed by the battalion that day to seventeen, without counting the guns and other gear. At Chênedollé, on August 7, SS-Uscha Fey's *Tiger* managed to destroy 15 *Shermans* in half an hour. The battalion had destroyed 24 additional enemy tank, which made fifty in the space of a few days.

The Tiger I at Vimoutiers, which belonged to the Schwere SS Panzer-Abteilung 102, was the only Panzer left in Normandy for years. This tank has gone into Second World War legend. Photo Rémy Desquesnes

The last battalion of *Tigers*, the *503.s Pz-Abt.*, entered the fray on July 10, the day after the *102.s* first involvement. *SS-Pz-Abt.* By July 11, not conceding a single loss, the *Tigers* burned ten *Shermans* at Colombelles. On July 18, the unit bore the brunt of the carpet bombing which preceded *Operation Goodwood* and one of the three companies was virtually wiped out; 5 *Tigers* were permanently destroyed. The *Tigers* fought in groups of 3 or 4, making them less identifiable by the Allied air forces. Ambush was the *Tiger* crews' favourite tactic, especially as the reach of their main armament was put to good use on the Caen plain. *Operation Goodwood* was very costly for the battalion, which lost its first *Königstiger* when it was rammed by a *Sherman*. On July 19, there were only 29 *Tigers*, left, of which nine were operational. The *101.s SS-Pz-Abt.* were also involved in *Operation Goodwood*, in the Bourguébus sector. There were only 25 *Tigers* left, of which six were operational.

At the beginning of August, the *Tigers* of the *102.s SS-Pz-Abt.* were opposing *Operation Bluecoat* near Mont Pinçon. On August 9, the battalion was sent to the Caen - Falaise road, The *503.s Pz-Abt* was also sent towards la Suisse Normande. On this occasion, a Tiger *II* was surprised in the middle of refuelling at Plessis-Grimoult and was destroyed by a mortar. The *101.s SS-Pz-Abt.* was engaged in the furious fighting in the plain between Caen and Falaise, where Montgomery was trying to carry the day during *Operations Totalise* and *Tractable*. As usual, the *Tigers* took a heavy toll on the crews of the Allied tanks. On August 8, Ekins, a *Firefly* sniper of the *33rd Armoured Brigade*, managed the feat of destroying three *Tigers* in twelve minutes, including No. 007, the 'mount' of the legendary Wittmann, who perished in it, with its entire crew.

The Tiger's camouflage can clearly be seen in this photograph. It was a formidable weapon when handled by an expert crew. The number 110 shows that it was a staff tank. This photograph was taken at Morgny, in the Eure, in the course of an exercise carried out in the spring of 1944: there are multi-coloured camouflage uniforms side by side with motorcyclists' waterproofs and cloth coats. The officer seen from the front, wearing camouflage uniform and carrying a black cap, is the battalion commander, Heinz von Westernhagen. DR

The 88 mm gun on this Tiger II, called the Königstiger (Royal Tiger), was impressive. No Allied tank could withstand it. Only twelve Tiger IIs were involved in the fighting in Basse-Normandie, where they did not exactly shine. PAC

Pushed back into the Falaise Pocket, few *Tigers* of the three *Schweres Panzer-Abteilungen* succeeded in escaping from the hell of Normandy and crossing the Seine. Most of them were destroyed, or sabotaged by their crews in various circumstances, usually due to a lack of fuel, ferries robust enough to transport them to the other bank of the Seine, or mechanical problems.

The fighting waged by *Tiger* tanks in Tunisia were the source of the legend of this armoured vehicle. The psychological impact on Allied veterans of the effect of *Tigers* in battle was considerable. Very often, the Allied reports mentioned the presence of *Tigers* even when no such armoured vehicle was present in the battle. The *Tiger,* too few of which were engaged, was capable of feats on the tactical plan, but had no decisive effect on the conduct of operations. This steel monster was handicapped by its weight, its excessive fuel consumption, its slowness and its overly delicate mechanisms, aggravated in the hedgerow field by the too-frequent changes of gear, which damaged the gearbox. The 88mm L/56 gun of the *Tiger I* and the 88mm L/71 of the *Königstiger* were capable of overcoming any Allied machine over very long distances. Particularly effective in ambush, especially in the Caen plain close to Falaise or around Hill 112 where the reach of its armament gave it a deadly advantage, like all armoured personnel carriers, the *Tiger* was less comfortable in the hedgerows or in urban warfare, in which short-range fighting overrode any superiority in armament. Nevertheless, the gains accredited to the battalions of heavy tanks in Normandy were particularly impressive. The score of *101.s SS-Pz-Abt.* had destroyed at least 200 Allied armoured cars. At August 22, the *102.s SS-Pz-Abt.* had destroyed 228 Allied tanks. Rapidly deprived of a company, and then facing the enemy in the *bocage*, the *503.s Pz-Abt.* only destroyed a hundred Allied tanks. If these claims turned out to be well-founded, this represented 14% of Allied tanks destroyed for barely 6% of *Panzers* committed, evidence - if need be - of the effectiveness of the *Tiger*.

Seventy years after having been abandoned by its crew, the Tiger at Vimoutiers is still impressive. One of 123 involved in Normandy, this powerful Panzer did not change the outcome of the battle. Photo T. Le Sant

243.Infanterie-Division

Formed in 1943, Generalleutnant Hellmich's *243. ID* supported the defence of the west coast of the Cotentin Peninsula from the month of April 1944 onwards. It had 11,529 men in its ranks. It was a strong unit, and its mobility was good, compared to similar units engaged in opposing the Allied invasion. In fact, its artillery batteries, equipped with Russian guns, were not horse-drawn but motorised. Its heavy anti-tank equipment was consistent, since it had ten *Sturmgeschützen*, fourteen *Marder IIIs* and nine *Pak 40*s. The unit was prepared to repel the invasion by carrying out several training exercises on the coast and inland, performing day and night exercises, while not neglecting the troop's political indoctrination. When the Landings took place, the *243.ID* was engaged against the bridgehead of *Utah Beach*. The tenacity of the resistance it offered in front of Montebourg allowed Collins' first attempt in the direction of Cherbourg to be countered. The *7th US Corps* therefore had first to weaken the opponent by isolating the great port. That was established on June 18, when the *GIs* seized Barneville. The day before, Hellmich had been killed. The *243.ID*, cut in two, lost part of its strength in the trap which had closed on Cherbourg.

Crouching in the *bocage*, stick grenades in his belt, this NCO of the 243. ID can quietly observe the enemy, using his camouflaged binoculars. The better to hide in the surrounding vegetation, he has stuck foliage into his helmet.
Coll. T. Le Sant

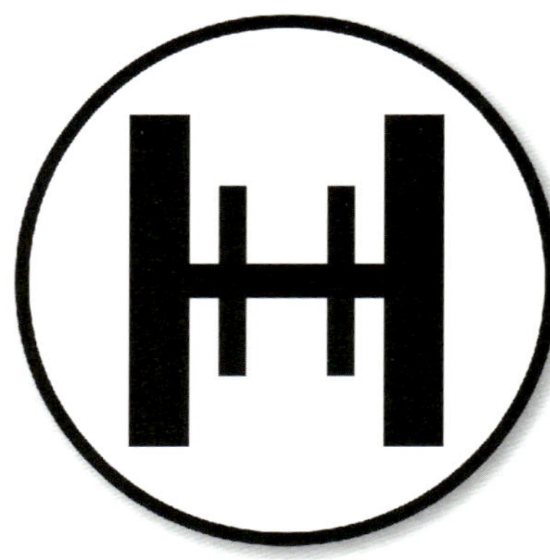

Insignia of the 243 Infanterie Division

A column of German prisoners in Cherbourg. Part of the 243. ID was isolated, then wiped out during the fighting for the great port. There was only one Kampfgruppe left in the line to the south of the Cotentin. NARA (© Editions Ouest-France - colorisation Graph&ti)

Oberst Klosterkemperer's *Kampfgruppe* had escaped being surrounded and was in the south of the Cotentin Peninsula, in the La Haye-du-Puits sector. The remains of *243.ID* were involved in a costly battle of the Hedgerows. The defence was effective, and led to vigorous counter-attacks, in spite of its limited means. In this kind of fighting, where it is easy to move and conceal, the mortar - which caused 70% of the Allied losses - proved particularly effective. Nevertheless, by July 11, the losses since June 6 were 8,186 men, and there were only 700 men in the front line trenches. On July 23 just before the launch of *Cobra*, the division had no more than four weak infantry battalions, three *Sturmgeschützen* and eight heavy anti-tank guns. When Bradley went on the offensive, the remains of the *243. ID* could only fold before the assault and the *Kampfgruppe*, finally surrounded in the Falaise Pocket, was wiped out there. The division had lost 10,000 men in the course of the campaign. It was dissolved in September 1944, and was never reconstituted.

THE TAKING OF CHERBOURG

The *7th US Corps* cut off the Cotentin Peninsula at its base by arriving on the west coast on June 18. The Cherbourg garrison and the disorganised remains of several divisions, placed under the command of Generalleutnant von Schlieben, the commander of the *709.ID,* fought to the limit of their strength. The Müller *Kampfgruppe,* from the *243.ID,* took the left wing of the Front between Vauville and Sainte-Croix-Hague, including the *Westeck* fortified area at Greville. It was in this sector that the *Gren. Rgt. 922* and two batteries of the *Art. Rgt. 243* fought until the final surrender. Deprived of the chance of reinforcements by land, the battle was hopeless for the Germans.

9th US Infantry Division « Varsity »

Reactivated in 1940 at Fort Bragg, where it underwent intensive training, the 9th US ID was one of the few experienced divisions which Eisenhower had available for Overlord, since it has fought in the Mediterranean. Its training was of excellent quality, beginning with its commanding officer, Major-General Eddy. Like the generals of the Wehrmacht, Eddy was a man who led his division from the front and did not hesitate to expose himself in the front line, from where he could quickly give the necessary orders. Attached to the 7th US Corps of Collins, the 9th US ID landed on Utah Beach on June 10. Its first offensive action consisted of cleaning up the enemy's coastal positions as far as Quinéville, on the right flank of the 4th US ID . However, this operation only involved a single regiment. It was on June 15 that the entire division took part in a large-scale attack. On June 18, it arrived in Barneville-Carteret and Portbail, on the west coast of the Cotentin. Eddy was then able to achieve a delicate manoeuvre for a division in contact with the enemy: he reoriented his units 90° towards the north. In twenty-two hours, his 20,000 men were again ready to get to work, the wounded and sick evacuated, the telephone lines laid, the depots redeployed and orders given in view of the assault on Cherbourg. This was launched on June 19. On June 26, the 9th US ID reached the Cherbourg arsenal. From June 29 until July 1, hard fighting allowed it to overcome the final resistance of Keil's Kampfgruppe at Cap de la Hague.

A welcome cigarette break for this GI in the 9th US ID, possibly a veteran of the fighting in the Mediterranean. Map-case, binoculars, Colt 45 and M1 rifle: everything to indicate an officer. The ideal target for a sniper!
Coll. T. Le Sant

The 9th US ID fought a hard battle for *Cobra*. Its commander, Manton Eddy, who can be seen here in his Jeep with his hand on the windscreen, had come to find out about the situation on the ground. Like the two officers with whom he is talking, there is very little in his appearance to betray the fact that he is an officer. This practice in the American army should not suggest that discipline was lacking. NARA (© Editions Ouest-France - colorisation Graph&ti)

The insignia of the 9th US ID "The Varisy". Coll. T. Le Sant

THE 9TH US ID ISOLATED THE PORT OF CHERBOURG

The first major success for the *9th US ID* in Normandy was surely to have cut the Cotentin Peninsula in two, as a prelude to the reduction of the *Festung* of Cherbourg. In so doing, the *GIs* decimated part of a still-intact German division: the *77.ID*. Tenacious and fresh, the *77.ID*, which has caused problems for the *Blues* of the *90th US ID*, was faced this time with the veterans of the *9th US ID*, whose thrust was irresistible. The *77.ID*, contrary to Hitler's orders, attempted to avoid being surrounded This withdrawal was, however, recommended by the *LXXXIV Korps* because of the impossibility to give logistical support to more than the *709.ID* and part of the *243. ID*, from the port of Cherbourg. On June 19, the *Gren. Rgt. 1050* of Oberst Bacherer managed to seize a bridge on the Ollande and part of the *77.ID* managed to forge a path towards the south, but at the cost of many losses, including almost all the artillery. The same day, Eddy's *9th US ID* began its offensive towards the north: objective Cherbourg.

By June 30, the 9th US ID had lost 2,438 men. Then the division's terrible Hedgerow War began. The GIs' struggle in the bocage was a gory disappointment for the Americans. The Germans, past masters in the art of defence and camouflage, showed their terrible effectiveness and demonstrated all their talents as combatants in this environment, where the Allied troops' numerical superiority and equipment was somewhat reduced, and where good training showed its full value. On July 9, the 9th US ID crossed the Taute and the Vire canal, pushing toward Tribehou and Le Dézert. Two days later, it was faced with the Panzer Lehr's counter-attack. The GIs only conceded 800 metres of ground and only lost 100 men before the fighter-bombers arrived. Thanks to this support, the GIs managed to regain the lost ground without difficulty. Progress towards the south, not in any way called into question by this counter-attack, resumed the next day.

The 9th US ID was in the front line for *Operation Cobra*. It was they who made the furthest breakthrough on July 25: the 47th Infantry Regiment seized Montreuil-sur-Lozon. Coll. T. Le Sant

The Hedgerow War required caution when advancing: the enemy could be close at hand. This photo was obviously not taken on the spot, but it clearly illustrates the ground that the 9th US ID had to cross to cut off the Cotentin peninsula. NARA

Two GIs of the 39th Infantry Regiment of the 9th US ID carefully survey the terrain. On June 23, the division entered the outskirts of Cherbourg before clearing the area around La Hague. NARA

On July 25, the division was in the front line for Operation Cobra Ninety-two men were hit by the carpet bombing, which was the preliminary to the offensive. This early setback in no way undermined its fighting spirit. Eddy made the best progress of the day, reaching Montreuil-sur-Lozon in spite of an ever-tenacious opponent. At the beginning of August, between Vire and Sourdeval, it was faced with various German counter-attacks aimed at restoring the situation. The division took part in the battle of the Falaise Pocket on the southern front in the Briouze sector while on August, 20 Eddy, promoted to Commander of the 12th US Corps, assigned his command to Craig.

The division subsequently took part in operations as far as Germany. In December 1944, when it was engaged in the fighting in the direction of the Roer dams, it had to face the German counter-offensive in the Ardennes. In March, it crossed the Rhine at Remagen where it took part in the fighting of the Ruhr Pocket. On May 8, 1945, it was located near Dessau.

Like most infantry divisions, the 9th US ID was attached to a battalion of M10 tank destroyers. The M10, however, suffered from armour-plating which was too thin, and the lack of a roof to its turret.
Photo: T. Le Sant

Osttruppen

The sleeve badge shows without any doubt that he is a soldier from the Osttruppen. Many officers, like this veteran holder of the Iron Cross and the Close Combat Clasp, were German. The arms were often disparate and included, as with this PPSH41 machine gun, Soviet weapons.
Coll. T. Le Sant

A soldier from an Osttruppen unit. If the camouflaged steel helmet and the uniform indicate that he was a member of the Wehrmacht, the headgear (a papascha) showed that he belonged to an Eastern unit. Russians, Cossacks, Turks and Ukrainians fought in Normandy.
Coll. T. Le Sant

It was by this term, literally 'the Eastern troops', that the Soviet citizens fighting alongside the German army were designated. The *Hiwis,* abbreviation of *Hilfwillige* - auxiliary volunteers - were the *Wehrmacht's* auxiliary personnel (drivers, cooks, sappers and logistics staff). Being a *Hiwi* allowed them to avoid the ill-treatment the Germans inflicted on their Soviet prisoners. Others, anti-Soviets, embraced the Nazi cause for political reasons. Similarly, battalions of *Osttruppen,* fighting units commanded by German officers, were engaged against partisans and the Red Army before being transferred to the Western front, in order to protect them from any risk of defection. Engaged in the fight against the Resistance, or even in tasks of occupation or surveillance, the *Osttruppen* were guilty - like the *Wehrmacht* and the *Waffen SS* - of a number of crimes against civilians. In January 1944, there were 65,000 Soviets in the ranks of the *Wehrmacht* in France, of whom 33,000 were fighting in Normandy. The *term Ostlegionnen* was also used. Many German divisions had at least one battalion of *Osttruppen* or even *Hiwis.* Their conduct in combat was very variable. Generally tenacious on the defensive, they proved to be unreliable when it came to conducting an attack. However, it should be emphasized that the arming of these units was often motley, largely of Russian origin and without heavy equipment. If the behaviour under fire of these battalions may have been satisfactory, as a general rule, they were units of poor quality, their motivation making them flawed. Some German officers would have been killed by *Osttruppen* seeking surrender. The start of a mutiny occurred even within the *Ost-Btl 795,* which fought near Isigny before disappearing to the south of Coutances. In the *Ost-Btl 797,* following a staff dispute, a Georgian officer murdered his superior, Hauptmann Massberg. On June 6, the Ukrainian Cossacks of the *Ost-Btl 441* as well as the Russians of the *Ost-Btl 642* showed a more combative face to the Canadians who disembarked at Courseulles-sur-Mer. Others opposed the landings on *Gold* and *Sword Beach,* or faced the paras of the 6th *Airborne,* in vain.

These two Turks were captured by British troops of the 51st ID in July 1944. On August 25, there were 25,000 Osttruppen among the prisoners held by the Allies. Their fate was unenviable: they were handed over to Stalin. IWM

FIGHTING IN THE COTENTIN

The divisions cut off in the Cotentin Peninsula had several battalions of *Osttruppen* or even *Hiwis.* The *77.ID* counted 1,410 *Hiwis* in its ranks. The *243.ID* included the *Ost-Btl 600,* made up of Russians. The *709.ID* included several Eastern units: the *Ost-Bataillonen 649, 561, 795* and *797.* If the first two battalions were trained by the Russians, the other two were composed of recruits of Georgian origin. These units disappear almost completely with the reduction of the *Festung* of Cherbourg. The *Ost-Btl 795,* which valiantly resisted the invasion, was isolated around Turqueville on the evening of June 6. The survivors fell back on Carentan and fought there alongside the *Fallschirmjäger.* The Americans did not hesitate to use psychological war fare by sending tracts into Huber's *Ost-Bataillon* Huber in position on the road to La Haye-du-Puits - Saint-Sauveur-le-Vicomte on July 3. In fact, the *Osttruppen's* resistance was not particularly determined during this gory American offensive at the beginning of the month of July.

15th Scottish Division

An efficient signalling system is absolutely essential for the success of an operation. This soldier of the Signals Corps, ready to give his all if necessary, therefore had a task of the utmost importance: he was charged with something on which the survival of his unit might depend. Coll. T. Le Sant

Formed in 1939, the *15th Scottish*, an extensively trained unit, remained on standby duty in the United Kingdom for four years before going into action. Although having no combat experience, the unit was dependable and extremely well trained. It had taken part in the most important manoeuvres which were held in the United Kingdom, including the exercises *Blackcock* and *Eagle*. The *Jocks*, the Scottish soldiers, were renowned for their courage and fighting spirit. The sound of the bagpipes encouraged the combatants, and strengthened their fighting spirit.

Their baptism of fire came during *Operation Epsom*, launched on June 26, just two days after the end of the division's landing commanded by Major-General MacMillan. The final failure of this offensive, which was very costly in human losses, could have permanently undermined the unit's morale. But the Scots showed their courage, and were actively engaged throughout the campaign. The *Jocks* were then involved in *Operation Greenline*, a diversion to take attention away from *Operation Goodwood*, from their bridgehead over the Odon. On July15, Esquay was taken, thanks to artificial moonlight created by the anti-aircraft searchlights, which also dazzled their opponents. However, the Scots and the supporting *Churchill Crocodiles* were thrown back from the village by the *Frunsbergs*. The *15th Scottish* broke through the enemy front during *Operation Bluecoat*, launched in late July. The *Jocks*, who had charged nine kilometres into enemy territory, seized the important Hill 309.

Operation Epsom. The 'Jocks' of the 7th Seaforth Highlanders are deployed in a field. The Scots' speed and fighting spirit allowed them to harvest successes right from the start of the offensive. Even with the support of the artillery and the tanks, it took a great deal of courage to throw themselves towards the enemy lines across the battlefield. IWM

Pipers were part of the legend of the Scottish troops (five per battalion). This June 25, the Jocks of the 7th Seaforth Highlanders advanced towards the Odon to the strains of the bagpipes ... IWM

A red lion rampant on a gold background: the emblem of the 15th Scottish Division. The tartan indicates that it is the 2nd Battalion of the Argyll and Sutherland Highlanders.
Coll. T. Le Sant

THE 'SCOTTISH CORRIDOR'

Engaged as first strike force for *Operation Epsom* on June 26 1944, the *15th Scottish* fulfilled its task with the support of the *31st Armoured Brigade* and *Churchill Crocodiles*, as well as a few *Sherman Flails*. If the Scots managed to push a salient into the German lines, they - the 'Scottish corridor' - remained narrow, and therefore vulnerable. The skilful defence of the *Waffen SS* was delayed, or even stopped, from making any progress on the wings of the offensive. On June 27, the Odon was crossed by the *Jocks*, who seized the bridge of Tourmauville. The taking of Gavrus strengthened the bridgehead south of the Odon. If the *11th Armoured Division* managed to take over Hill 112, this position remained too exposed. The pincer attack of *I.* and *II. SS Panzerkorps*, on the flanks of the 'Scottish corridor' threatened the division. The *2nd Argyll and Sutherland Highlanders* was severely hit by a counter-attack from the *Frunsberg* on Gavrus. The *Jocks*, supported by fire from *HMS Roberts*, only abandoned the bridge under orders. At Grainville, the *8th Royal Scots* resisted the opposition of the *Kampfgruppe* commanded by Weidinger, of the *Das Reich*. Montgomery, noting the failure of *Epsom*, put an end to the offensive and also ordered the abandoning of Hill 112. The *Scots* had been put to a terrible test in the dogged fighting for the crossing of the Odon. It cost them 2,720 men between June 25 and July 2, that is, a quarter of the losses which were inflicted on them during the war.

After a week of bloody clashes around Hill 226 and Estry, the division, which had been commanded by Major-General Barber since August 5, was allowed to rest, then resumed its march east, which took them beyond Gacé. The Seine was crossed on the 27th.

The *Jocks* penetrated into Belgium on September 6, then the Netherlands on the 17th of the same month. The division fought until February 1945 when it marched into Germany. On March 24, they crossed the Rhine, then advanced to the north of Germany. On May 8, they were between Hamburg and Lübeck. The division's losses, since June 6 1944, had risen to 11,772 men

Bren Carriers of the 1st Middlesex Regiment progress behind a Sherman 'Crab' in the summer heat of July 30, 1944. *Operation Bluecoat* took place on a hilly terrain with scattered woods and hedges, very favourable to the defenders. Coll. particulière

THE ARMOURED BRIGADES

During the battle of Normandy, the *15th Scottish Division* operated in conjunction with several independent armoured units. These last were derived from a very special design of British armoured car. The *Royal Armoured Corps* differentiated between its *Armoured Divisions,* supplied with tanks whose design placed its emphasis on speed and mobility, in the image of the cavalry of yesteryear, and its *Independent Armoured Brigades,* units whose main function was to provide support to the armoured infantry formations. Unlike the armoured divisions, the *Independent Armoured Brigades* only had tank regiments, three in number, with a total of 220 tanks, 1,000 vehicles and 3,400 men. Seven *Independent Armoured Brigades* were engaged in Normandy: the *6th Guards, 31st, 33rd* and *34th Army Tank Brigades* (equipped mainly with *Churchills,* the infantry tank then being issued) and the *4th, 8th* and *27th Armoured Brigades* (these last two having received *Sherman DD* amphibious tanks, with a view to D-Day). Most often split up in their engagements, these armoured brigades - nearly 1,500 tanks - provided essential support to the infantry divisions of the *21st Army Group.*

9.SS Panzerdivision « Hohenstaufen »

The insignia of the 9.SS Panzerdivision 'Hohenstaufen'.

Commanded by SS-Gruppenführer Bittrich, this division was raised in France in February 1943 and set off for the Eastern front, where it took part in the fighting at Tarnopol in March 1944 beside the *Frunsberg*, the other division of the *II.SS Panzerkorps*. From June 12, the division was recalled to the West. It was, therefore, a unit with experience gained from its fighting in the East which arrived in Normandy. It lacked a quarter of its officers and under-officers, did not have an anti-tank battalion and suffered from a considerable deficit of all-terrain transport capacity. Its strength was satisfactory, since the division had 20,910 men with the *Hiwis*, as well as 168 *Panzers* and *Sturmgeschützen*. This last figure should not hide the fact that the crews had not been able to benefit from adequate training on the *Panthers*, which had only just been issued.

This Panzergrenadiere is wearing a feldgrau (field grey) overall with the characteristics SS runes, seen on the left side of his helmet. He wears an eagle on his left sleeve, not the right, above the chest, as on the German Wehrmacht uniform.

Coll. T. Le Sant

The Wespe, carrying a 105 mm gun, was the standard self-propelled artillery piece in the Panzer-Divisionen . The Hohenstaufen had twelve within two batteries. They also had six self-propelled 150mm Hummels, and 28 field guns, which was unusual for a armoured division. Coll. T. Le Sant

A 1944 model Sdkfz 250, simplified as compared to earlier models so as to increase production. These devices were particularly used by reconnaissance units. The three-tone camouflage was very common in Normandy, but far from being in general use. It came in several patterns. Photo T. Le Sant

RAURAY

As a front for *Operation Epsom,* the *12th British Corps* triggered *Operation Martlet* on June 25. The *49th West Riding* pushed back the *Panzer Lehr* and the *Hitlerjügend,* who were supported by *Tigers,* then seized Fontenay-le-Pesnel and Rauray on June 27. Two days later, the *Hohenstaufen* counter-attacked, trying to threaten the flank of *Epsom* with its objectives Rauray and Cheux. The *Waffen SS* surprised Allied units in the course of being relieved. Grainville-sur-Odon fell before being retaken by the British. Getting the units into place was delayed by the harassment of the Allied air forces and the bombardment of the *Royal Navy.* Rauray was the scene of a fierce battle which lasted until July 2. The *Panzers,* deceived by dummy guns and *Sherman* carcasses, fell prey to anti-tank weapons, which destroyed them at short range. The *'Victor Targets'* - concentrated firing of all the artillery of a British Army corps - and indiscriminate mortar shelling definitively ruined any hope of success for the Germans. A unit of *Panzer* elite, supported by other formations, had therefore failed in its confrontation with an infantry division, the *49th West Riding Division.*

There are smiles on the faces of this SS tank crew: they had not yet lived through the hell of Normandy. The man in the foreground is refreshing himself from his billy-can. The additional armoured skirts (Schürzen) of the Panzer IV gave it a more massive silhouette, closer to that of the Tiger I - leading to many mistakes. DR

While Rommel hoped to have the two *SS* divisions of the *II.SS Panzerkorps* available to push the Allies back to the sea, he was forced to engage them in the battle of the Odon. The *9.SS* had to counter-attack on Rauray. From then on, the *Hohenstaufen*, far from constituting the spearhead of a decisive counter-offensive, became bogged down in a war of positions, very costly in men and equipment By July 1, there were already 1,168 men, 32 *Panzers* and *Sturmgeschützen* and 18 guns out of action. The losses in the ranks of the infantry were such that the two *Panzergrenadiere* regiments had to be amalgamated to form just one. In July, the *Hohenstaufen* took part in the terrible fighting of Hills 112 and 113, which cost them 1,891 men. However, it had captured 67 enemy tanks, including 11 in working condition.

Then deployed on the right bank of the Orne, in support of the *271.ID*, two of its *Kampfgruppen* successfully opposed the *Spring* offensive, launched towards May-sur-Orne by the Canadians on July 25. Kluge was not, therefore, able to place *Panzer* units in reserve. By taking the division south of Caen again, it was well away from the American zone, from which *Operation Cobra* was launched that day, July 25. By July 31, 47 *Panzers* and *Sturmgeschützen* had been destroyed, while 79 remain operational.

At the beginning of August, after a month of fighting in south-west of Caen, the unit had to intervene in the Vire and Estry region, to oppose the British breakthrough generated by *Operation Bluecoat*. On August 16, it withdrew to the east, and took up a position around Vimoutiers. It could not prevent the Polish and Canadians from blockading the Falaise pocket. It was from this sector that it counter-attacked, together with the *Das Reich* so as to allow the evacuation of encircled units. In this way, it formed a collecting line for the troops escaping from the trap. The Normandy campaign cost about 5,000 men in the division, but there were no more than 460 *Panzergrenadiere* by August 21.

The *Hohenstaufen's* hour of glory occurred a month later, in September 1944, when, sent to rest in the Netherlands and on the point of departure for Germany, it contributed - even though considerably reduced - to the failure of the Allied airborne operation *Market Garden* in the Arnhem and Nijmegen sectors. Restored to strength, it took part in the Battle of the Bulge and then the *Wehrmacht's* last offensive, in Hungary in March 1945.

Number of operational *Panzer* and *Panzerjäger*

June 1	109
July 5	67
August 6	27
August 21	20 - 25

10.SS Panzerdivision « Frunsberg »

SS Brigadeführer Harmel, aboard a command Sdkfz 251 - recognisable by its tubular antenna - chatting with some of his officers. The division suffered terribly in its first engagement.
Bundesarchiv

Raised in France in February 1943, the *Frunsberg*, commanded by SS-Brigadeführer Harmel, was essentially made up of young recruits. In March 1944, despite being the *OKW's* reserve in the event of an Allied landing, the *II.SS Panzer-korps* left France for Poland, and met the Russians at Tarnopol. On June 12, the unit was recalled to France. The *Frunsberg* division was particularly poorly endowed, since it lacked a tank battalion and its anti-tank battalion. Its *Panzergrenadiere* regiments were not at full strength either. It only mustered approximately 16,000 men and 77 *Panzer IVs* and *Sturmgeschützen.*

Handicapped by supply difficulties, it took part in the fighting on the Odon and on Hill 112. Its counter-attack on Baron did not meet with success. 571 Men and two permanently destroyed *Panzers* were lost in the course of *Operation Epsom.* Their losses amounted to 2,289 men by July 18. After a month of fighting, the definitive losses of *Panzers* and *Sturmgeschützen* were limited to ten, which had been permanently destroyed. Early in August, the *Frunsberg* faced the British, who were trying to break through towards la Suisse Normande. The counter-attack achieved no more than a few tactical successes, such as that of August 2 when twenty British tanks were destroyed.

Insignia of the 10.SS Panzerdivision 'Frunsberg'.

On August 9, after a redeployment southwards to counter the Americans, the division attacked towards Barenton. Near Domfront, the pressure was such that the *Frunsberg* could not disengage to confront the *15th US Corps* which, further east, threatened the *VII. Army* with encirclement, in the direction of Argentan. As at August 14, the losses in armoured personnel carriers were then no more than 20. The division still represented a formidable foe. However, the number of combatants continued to decrease, and it underwent further losses in the Falaise pocket, from which it escaped bled dry after having conducted a brilliant rearguard action. It managed to cross the Seine at Oissel between August 25 and 27, but without a single armoured car. Its losses in the Campaign were at least 5,000 men.

It was a very much reduced unit which victoriously faced the Allied paratroopers and the *30th British Corps* in Nijmegen in September 1944. In January 1945, reinforced and re-equipped, the *Frunsberg* took part in the *Nordwind* offensive in Alsace. Transferred to the front of the Vistula, it surrendered to the Soviets in Saxony.

With its low profile, the Sturmgeschütze III made a more difficult target than the Panzer, and was easier to hide. However, the elevation of its gun was limited because of the turret, and the machine was often too low to be able to open fire above the level of the hedges. Coll. P. Tiquet

Number of operational *Panzer* and *Panzerjäger*

June 1	66
July 7	52
August 6	20
August 21	0

The 10. SS. The SS Frunsberg left the Eastern Front after having suffered losses. It had only 80 tanks, including 39 Panzer IVs, the model seen in this photograph, with its Schürzen (extra side armour-plating). The 1st. Battalionhad fallen, so the division had no Panthers. Coll. P. Tiquet

HILL 112

In the course of *Operation Epsom,* the *11th Armoured Division* managed to seize Hill 112, a strategic height which dominated the valley of the Odon, but more importantly that of the Orne. The view covered the defences established by the Germans to the south of Caen. Having had to abandon their untenable positions on Hill 112, the British launched *Operation Jupiter* on July 10. The *Frunsberg,* supported by *Tigers,* was more heavily engaged on Maltot, as well as on the positions which had been taken by the *43rd Wessex Division* right on the summit of Hill 112. The counter-attack led by the *SS* during the night of July 10 -11 was repelled, after particularly fierce fighting. The *II. SS Panzerkorps* struggled tenaciously, however, and once again forced its opponents to fall back: the survivors of the *5th Duke of Cornwalls* withdrew under the protection of the *Royal Scots Grey's Sherman.* The summit of Hill 112, under fire by the artillery of both camps, became a *no-man's land.*

16.Luftwaffe-Feld-Division

This Jäger of the 16. Luftwaffe-Feld -Division is wearing the camouflaged jacket typical of ground troops in the German air force. His trousers and jacket are in a blue-grey material. His helmet has also been camouflaged. He is carrying the simple German soldier's standard equipment.
Coll. T. Le Sant

The *16.Luft. Div.* of Generalmajor Sievers, formed from Luftwaffe ground crew units and trained by officers of the *Heer,* left its cantonment area in the Netherlands in June 1944. It was a still incomplete division which was dug in from Herouville to Cambes-en-Plaine from July 2 onwards. On June 26, a report of the *VII. Army* estimated it as being of poor quality, since the best elements of the *Luftwaffe* had joined the *Fallschirmjäger* or the air squadrons, apart from which its infantry battalions were limited to 500 men. Certainly, with 9,354 men in its ranks at the end of May 1944, its strength was reduced, but each regiment had six anti-tank guns and 18 *Panzerschreck.* The anti-tank battalion also had two *Sturmgeschützen* and nine *Paks,* not counting the *Flak* guns. On 8 July, it received eight additional *Sturmgeschützen* in reinforcement. The divisional artillery had twenty-four 76.2 and 122 mm. Russian guns.

The speedy emplacement of a 20 mm Flak gun. The effects of this weapon when fired on a land target were devastating. The photograph was taken at the end of August, at Drocourt, near Mantes, when the Americans had already crossed the Seine, and the 7.Arme Kutte (struggled) to extricate itself from the 'cauldron' of Falaise. DR

The Jäger established a defensive position to the north (*Operation Charnwood*, as on this picture) then to the east of Caen (*Operation Goodwood*) and fought with determination. Nonetheless, the division was virtually destroyed, then disbanded. Archives du Calvados

OPERATION *WINDSOR*

On July 8, the *2nd KSLI* of the *185th Brigade* managed to seize Lébisey wood, to which access had been prohibited by the German defenders since June 6. The task was arduous, faced with the defence of the *III/31. Jäger-Regiment* supported by a few *Panzer IVs* of the *21.Panzer*. The *Jäger* eventually retreated, and the *31. Jäger-Regiment* command post fell into British hands. The situation was in keeping with the entire front. Battered by two days of heavy artillery bombardment, the *16.Luft. Div.* fell back. 75% of the strength engaged by the *16.Luft. Div.* were lost, but the bulk of the division had not yet entered the lists.

A helmet - Schirmmütze - belonging to an officer of the Luftwaffe. The grey-blue material, the wings on either side of the roundel and the oak leaves, as well as the design of the eagle: it boasts all the characteristics of Luftwaffe headgear. Coll. T. Le Sant

From July 7, the *Jäger* of the *16.Luft. Div.* bore the brunt of the hail of iron and fire of *Operation Charnwood.* If the bombardment only hit the front lines, however, the *16.Luft. Div.* had to concede the Caen left bank, to establish a new line of defence between the Bois de Bavent and the steelworks at Colombelles. Rear-guard units, including snipers, nevertheless contributed to carrying out a delaying action north of Caen. Despite everything, the decimated division had not lost any of its aggression. On July 11, the *Jäger* faced up to the *51th Highland* in front of the Colombelles steelworks. Ten of the *33th British Armoured Brigade's Shermans* fell under the *Tigers'* attack.

On July 18, the *16.Luft. Div.* was once again in the dress circle for a major Allied offensive: *Operation Goodwood.* The intensive artillery preparation managed to weaken the *Jäger* who, dazed by the carpet bombing which had cut down their lines, were incapable of stopping the enemy's advance. Combat groups, provided with collective weapons and with the support of anti-tank guns, especially the self-propelled

units of the *21.Panzerdivision*, still showed tremendous fighting spirit, sometimes only giving in after a bitter struggle. Nevertheless, the division came out of the confrontation bled white. With the loss of 2,500 men, the *16.Luft. Div.* had almost no infantrymen left. The losses of officers were such that the unit had to be dissolved on August 4, the survivors being sent to the *21.Panzerdiv.*, the *346.Infantry Div* . and the *272.Infantry Div.*

The Jäger and gunners of the Luftwaffe wear camouflage uniforms. Their helmets were often painted in several shades, or covered with net, which gave them the look of elite troops. Often disparaged, they fought with a degree of success outside Caen, in the Eure and on the Seine. DR

The Flak Cannon, here an anti-aircraft 20 mm gun, was normally the only one associated with the Luftwaffe ground forces. There were, however, two infantry divisions (16. and 17. Luftwaffe-Feld -Divisionen) involved in the battle of Normandy. Coll. T. Le Sant

A Jäger taking cover in a manhole. He had camouflaged his helmet to blend into the environment. This soldier was particularly well equipped to ensure a warm welcome for the British, with a Panzerfaust and several stick grenades. Mémorial de Caen

The young recruits of the Luftwaffe-Feld-Divisionen were in fact the Luftwaffe ground crew. Infantry combat training was inadequate and the quality of supervision was lacking. Nevertheless, in Normandy, their bearing under fire was more effective than it had been reported. Coll. T. Le Sant

Guards Armoured Division « Open Eye Division »

This officer of the Guards Armoured Division is wearing the cap typical of officers in the British army. On his belt, he is carrying the equipment (in canvas webbing) appropriate to his rank: case for binoculars, compass case . . .
Coll. T. Le Sant

Major-General Adair's *Guards Armoured Division* - 15,000 men, 290 tanks, 360 armoured personnel carriers, 270 guns - was raised in June 1941 from the prestigious elite troops which formed the units of the *Guards.* Was its long and careful training, and its discipline when faced with any ordeal, sufficient to make it into a division capable of dealing serious blows against a seasoned enemy? This shortcoming was all the more significant since the cooperation between the infantry and the armoured cars, essential in the confrontation to come, seemed to have been neglected. The storm which had broken over the Channel delayed its transfer to Normandy until June 22.

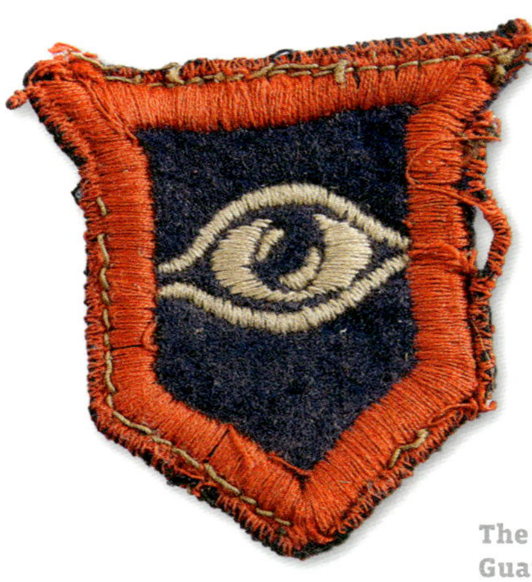

The insignia of the Guards Armoured Division, the 'Ever Open Eye' Division.
Coll. T. Le Sant

Some Guards soldiers and their light vehicles at the rear of the Front. An armoured division does not only include tanks. It is in fact a small-scale army with its logistics unit, supply corps, workshops, etc.
Coll. T. Le Sant

OPERATION *GOODWOOD*

Engaged at second level after the *11th Arm. Div.,* the *Guards,* held up by the congestion which had seized the channels of communication in the narrow bridgehead to the east of the Orne, were able to join battle from early in the afternoon of July 18. The division was unable to obtain tangible results against an effective opponent on the defensive, and armed with anti-tank weapons whose long range allowed him to inflict significant losses. These losses around Cagny and Vimont were serious, and the cost was sixty-six tanks. The division distinguished itself, however, by an exceptional feat of arms: a section leader in the *Irish Guards,* Lieutenant Gorman managed to destroy first a *Tiger I* and then a *Tiger II* at Émiéville, after having rammed the second. These were the first *Königstigers* to be destroyed by the Allies.

Tommies take shelter in the embankment of a hedge, Bren machine-gun at the ready. As in the enemy camp, they have camouflaged their helmets, the better to blend into the vegetation. The enemy must be far away, otherwise the exposed position of the two officers in the background is hard to explain. They are close to Cagny, on July 18, and these men belong to the Guards Armoured Division. PAC

The night before *Operation Goodwood*, July 17. A column of Bren Carriers of the 1st (Motor) Grenadier Guards, 5th Guards Brigade, is crossing 'Euston Bridge' over the Orne at Ranville. The Guards Armoured Division would spearhead the attack but these infantrymen, busy clearing the ground, lacked tanks. This signals half-track belonged to the command post of a battalion. Two men are wearing protective goggles: the battlefield would soon be nothing but dust and smoke. IWM

On July 18, *Operation Goodwood* brought the *Guards Arm. Div.* into the field. Too much inflexibility in the command and a lack of initiative on the part of the officers did not allow the division to give the best of itself during this offensive, which Montgomery had hoped would be decisive. After a brief period of rest and rehabilitation, the *Guards Arm. Div.* was engaged in *Operation Bluecoat.* The British armoured weapons attempted to respond to the failures noted during its previous battles. The division was reorganized into combat groups combining infantry and armoured personnel carriers. These tactical groupings were given the title of *Bocage Battle Groups.* The stubborn defence and the force of the *Panzer* counter-attacks, however, limited the *Guards*' territorial gains during *Operation Bluecoat.* The Germans were still not defeated, and proved it at the expense of the *Guards Arm. Div.* in the Estry - Chênedolle sector, as well as on August 11 when a disaster befell its leading units at Sourdevalle.

In mid-August, Montgomery placed the division on reserve; it then participated in the clearing out of the Falaise pocket. The unit crossed the Seine River from August 29 onwards. It liberated Brussels before forming the spearhead of the land forces involved in *Operation Market Garden.* After an autumn and winter of fighting, mainly spent in the Netherlands, the *Guards* finished the war in the north of Germany. The liberation of the Bergen-Belsen concentration camp was, for many soldiers, the most terrible experience of the war.

A column of Guards infantrymen makes its way along a Norman road. The front line is far away, so these soldiers have taken off their helmets to wear the 'Cap Comforter'. Their equipment, made of webbing, can clearly be seen, especially their cartridge pouches, which were very much in the way when they had to fling themselves to the ground. IWM

The Guards took part in *Operation Bluecoat,* which allowed the German front line, already shaken by *Cobra,* to be pushed back. This column of Shermans, belonging to the 2nd Irish Guards and led by a lightly-armoured Stuart - a tank which was by then obsolete - was photographed south of Caumont on July 31. IWM

Units of the Guards at Cagny: the church can be recognised in the background. The fighting was very hard and costly in this sector. The division was at the head of the *Goodwood* offensive which constituted its baptism of fire. The losses in armoured personnel carriers were heavy but the advance obtained was still honourable, given the circumstances. DR

1.SS Panzerdivision « Leibstandarte Adolf Hitler »

Formed from Hitler's personal guard, this unit was in all the campaigns. Elevated to the rank of armoured division in 1943, it took part in the battles of Kharkov, Kursk and Zhitomir on the Eastern front. The division had been at rest in Belgium since April 1944, when the announcement of the Allied invasion was made. In the meantime, part of its strength was sent to the *Hitlerjügend* division, as officers. On June 6, 1944, the division commanded by SS-Brigadeführer Wisch had 19,618 men. There were only 133 *Panzers* and *Sturmgeschützen* on June 1, of which barely 124 were in operational condition. However, with the reinforcements it received, 225 were soon operational within the division in Normandy. The situation was similar with regard to its other vehicles (1,070 lorries in working condition out of 3,887 theoretically supplied) although the situation improved before it went to the front.

This tank crew member is wearing a leather Kriegsmarine uniform. On the chest, he bears the assault tank insignia, awarded to those who have taken part in three armoured assaults in the space of three days. Coll. T. Le Sant

These three soldiers of the Leibstandarte Adolf Hitler relish a few moments of rest. After the terrible Russian Front, it was the hell of the Battle of Normandy, in the course of which the division did not particularly shine. Coll. T. Le Sant

THE BOURGUÉBUS RIDGE

The *Leibstandarte Adolf Hitler* was positioned along the Orne, or in reserve south of Caen, when *Goodwood* was launched. Units of the division's reconnaissance arrived on Bourguébus Ridge around midday. The *Panthers* arrived shortly afterwards, taking the dominant position and operating, for once, with the company and not in isolated tanks, as they had operated in the hedgerows. Towards Four and Bourguébus, however, they risked an advance which was spotted, and was within enemy range. The losses incurred by the fanatical *SS* were terrible. The *Panzergrenadiere* of *III./SS- Pz-Gren.-Regt 1,* hidden in the wheat fields, were decimated at Bras and Hubert-Folie . The *Panzerfäuste* firing ignited the wheat, while the English machine-guns mowed the *SS* down. The *Sturmgeschütze* battalion, which had left its position on the Orne, also suffered heavy losses. On July 20, when Montgomery put an end to the offensive, out of 45 *Sturmgeschützen,* only 19 were operational, and only 71 *Panzer*s as against 105 three days earlier. Entrenched on Bourguebus Ridge, particularly in the woods of La Hogue near Garcelles-Secqueville, the division prevented all Allied progress towards Tilly-la-Campagne on July 25.

Insignia of the 1.SS Panzerdivision 'Liebstandarte Adolf Hitler'

On June 9, fearing a possible second Landing in the Pas-de-Calais, the decision taken the previous day to send operational elements to Normandy was cancelled: it was not until June 17 that its marching orders were received. The division arrived at the front in a very scattered formation, the units being engaged on arrival to counter *Operation Epsom.* On July 6, 14,000 men were ready to face the invasion, while 5,800 were still in Belgium; some units did not reach the Normandy front before the month of August. The *LAH* was operational to the south of Caen and faced the British armoured cars during *Operation Goodwood.*

The Panzer IV was the workhorse of all the German armoured divisions in 1944. The 1. SS Panzer deployed 103 of them in Normandy, along with 72 Panthers. However, the war in Normandy was nothing like the Eastern Front: all the tactics had to be reviewed. Coll. P. Tiquet

When it returned from the Russian Front to be resupplied in Belgium, the LAH sorely lacked armoured personnel carriers. As in other SS divisions, the Sturmgeschütze complemented the striking force of the Panzer. There were 45 of them in a battalion on June 1,1944.
Coll. T. Le Sant

Early in August, the *1.SS Panzer* was relieved by the *89.ID* and was sent west to take part in the Mortain counter-offensive. It still represented a formidable force. But the field, unfavourable to armoured cars, lent itself admirably to the defence. Speedily blocked before Juvigny-Tertre by a regiment of US infantry, the *LAH* did not distinguish itself during *Operation Lüttich.* On August 20, trapped in the Falaise pocket, command passed to SS-Brigadeführer Mohncke. Between August 19 and 21, leading the assault at the head of the column with the energy of despair, the *1.SS Panzer* managed to break through by way of Saint-Lambert-sur-Dive, but at the cost of heavy losses. The division no longer had a single operational tank, nor any artillery weapons. Its total losses in Normandy can be estimated at being in the order of 5,000 to 6,000 men.

Reorganized and restored to condition, it became the spearhead of the *VI. Panzerarmee* during the Ardennes offensive, during which many acts of violence were carried out in the wake of the advance of Peiper's *Kampfgruppe.* After the failure of the offensive, it participated in operations around Budapest and Lake Balaton, then finished the war in Steyr.

Number of operational *Panzer* and *Panzerjäger*

June 1	124
July 9	132
August 6	130
August 22	0

A Tiger I column of the Schwere SS Panzer-Abteilung 101 negotiates the bends near Morgny on June 7 1944: they had to get to the front line of the invasion! Members of the unit came from the 'Liebstandarte Adolf Hitler', but the heavy tank battalion formed part of the 1.SS Panzercorps, and no longer belonged to the 1.SS Panzer-Division.
Bundesarchiv.

III. Flak-Korps

This soldier of the III. Flak-Korps is wearing a Feldbluse bearing collar insignia on a red background as well as shoulder tabs edged with the same colour: he is, therefore, a gunner. At this time, the police helmet - the Feldmütze - was increasingly being replaced by a cap in the same fabric. Coll. T. Le Sant

If the Lutfwaffe was numerically outclassed in the air, Flak represented a danger for the Allied squadrons. The III. Flak-Korps, fully motorised, was deployed in Normandy to counter the invasion. Commanded by Generalmajor Pickert, it consisted of 1, 2, 3 and 4 Flak-Sturm-Regimenter, made up of 12,000 men, a hundred and eight 88mm guns (Flak 18/36/ 37/41) and 104 small arms on June 23. As the Flak-Sturm-Regiment 1 was deployed in the Bessin on June 6, the other regiments had to undertake the perilous push up from the Somme estuary.. On June 11, the corps' missions were defined, in anticipation of a mass counter-attack of Panzerdivisionen. The III. Flak-Korps had to secure the protection of the areas of concentration and the artillery batteries, as well as the probable attack zone of the I. SS Panzerkorps. Other Flak units of the Luftwaffe aided the German forces engaged in Normandy, including Flak-Gruppe Höhne of the 13.Flak-Division,which had its Command Post at Laval.

Extremely well camouflaged, this 20mm Flak 38 would not be spotted by Allied planes before opening fire. The position adopted here nevertheless suggests that the gun could be also used to fire along the ground - an exercise which is not as easy as it sounds, for gunners trained to fight planes. DR

The Flakvierling 38 with its four 20mm barrels was a formidable weapon against low-flying fighters. Used on land targets, it could cause chaos in an infantry formation. The corps received 12 of these guns as replacements during the battle. Coll. P. Tiquet

In early August, with the American breakthrough, this division received its orders to deploy its batteries between Mortain and St- Hilaire-du-Harcouët.

By going to the front, despite its anti-aircraft function, Pickert's corps suffered serious losses under the Jabos attack: 20 guns, 300 men, and 200 vehicles. Considerable reinforcements were supplied during the battle: fifty-four 88mm guns, thirty-six 37mm and eighty-four 20mm (twelve of which were quad-mounted Flakvierling). The corps fulfilled its anti-aircraft role, and claimed the destruction of 462 enemy aircraft. If the 88mms were effective against bombers when they opened fire on the regiment, Jabos were the target of the light Flak guns. 210,000 rounds of 88mm, 272,000 of 37mm and 2,716,000 of 20mm were fired. Its role as artillery support for land operations was also successful. Apart from the Flak-Sturm-Regiment 1, the III. Flak-Korps was predominantly engaged against the British sector, to the east of Caen. 5,777 men were lost, from Normandy until the end of the retreat in Germany June 23. The III. Flak-Korps was reconstituted in the Rhineland and participated - not without distinction - at the Battle of the Bulge. It was destroyed in the Ruhr Pocket.

Number of anti-aircraft guns within the *Flak-Sturm-Regimenter*

June 23	108 of 88 mm and 104 of 20 and 37 mm
August 8	116 of 88 mm and 160 of 20 and 37 mm

OPERATION *GOODWOOD*

If 88mm *Flak* guns were frequently used - successfully - in an anti-tank role on all fronts, the 88mms issued to the *III. Flak-Korps* were seldom committed against armoured targets. The Allies, however, had a strong propensity to identify the smaller opposing shot as being those of an 88mm gun. Pickert's corps only claimed the destruction of 14 Allied armoured vehicles and 92 tanks (out of almost 3,500 which the Wehrmacht believed it had destroyed in Normandy), of which 12 were victims of *Panzerfaüste* close protection units. Compared to the 88mm *Pak 43* and *Pak 43/41* designed as anti-tank guns, the 88mm *Flak* had the disadvantage of excessive weight and a high silhouette, which was difficult to conceal. Pickert, however, trained three *Flakkampfgruppen* for the fight against the tanks. The crews were poorly trained, and their results remained disappointing: 20 tanks destroyed for the loss of thirty-five 88mm guns as well as 70 small arms. During *Operation Goodwood,* significant losses to the British armoured vehicles (225 tanks) have long been wrongly attributed to the presence of the *III. Flak-Korps.* Apart from the single battery of four 88mm guns positioned at Cagny, it is highly unlikely that any other units of the corps opened fire on tanks during *Operation Goodwood.*

2nd Canadian Infantry Division

Raised in 1940, Major-General Foulkes' *2nd Canadian Infantry Division* was operationally engaged for the first time during the disastrous *Operation Jubilee* launched in the Dieppe sector in August 1942. In terms of quality, it never fully recovered from this defeat.

Its first engagement in Normandy was *Operation Atlantic*, on July 18. The Canadians managed to establish a bridgehead at Vaucelles, on the right bank of Caen, which had not yet been liberated. They entered Cormelles-le-Royal, Ifs, Fleury and Louvigny and reached Saint-Martin-de-Fontenay and the Verrières ridge, which it could not, however, maintain. The attack was particularly costly, since 1,349 losses, including 249 deaths, occurred. The *2nd Can. Div.* returned to the fray on July 25, in *Operation Spring*. It was another failure.

The Canadian soldier is equipped with exactly the same equipment as his British comrade, including the tin mug hanging from his haversack. The Mark III helmet, the turtle, on the other hand, was fairly widespread within the Canadian formations while most of the British still wore the Mark I tin helmet. Coll. T. Le Sant

The insignia of the 2nd Canadian Division: just as simple as that of the 3rd, just a dark blue rectangle. Coll. T. Le Sant

A 5.5" gun opens fire in the plain of Caen. Artillery was an essential weapon among the Allied forces. The 2nd Canadian ID had to fight hard to seize the right bank at Caen, then in its advance toward Falaise. PAC

OPERATION *SPRING*

Lieutenant General Simonds, commander of the *2nd Canadian Corps,* intended to maintain the surprise effect for the offensive and therefore decided to attack at night, taking advantage of the artificial moonlight given by the anti-aircraft searchlights. In addition, to conceal the direction of progress from the enemy, the artillery carried out saturation bombardment at specific targets, rather than its usual tactic of rolling fire. Cleverly concealed and entrenched, supported by reserves of *Panzer SS* and taking advantage of the mineshafts to spring on the assailants' rear, the German combatants repelled the Canadians, who suffered heavy losses. The latter, whose attacks were poorly coordinated, were decimated by machine guns and mortars in the wheat fields. With 324 losses, the *Black Watch of Canada* was wiped out. Foulkes lost 1,202 fighting men, of which 362 were killed. He was personally reprimanded by Simonds for the final failure of the operation.

The division also included French Canadian units, such as the Maisonneuve regiment. Coll. T. Le Sant

The division then prepared for *Operation Totalize*, launched on the night of August 6 - 7. The Canadians, progressing in four columns, finally seized the Verrières ridge, Rocquancourt and Bretteville-sur-Laize. A company of *Essex Scots* was reduced to 30 men, and lost 14 half-tracks. The *Mont-Royal Fusiliers* also suffered in front of May-sur-Orne, which only fell with the support of the *Churchill Crocodiles*. In the course of *Operation Tractable*, launched on August 14, the Canadians established a bridgehead beyond the Lizon. The *2nd Can. Div.* made its entry into Falaise on the afternoon of August 16th. The clearing of the ruins, in which a few *Waffen SS* fanatics were still hanging on, dragged on through the whole of August 17.

Foulkes then directed his unit towards the Seine. After hard fighting against the German rear-guard in the forest of La Londe from August 27 to 29, the division entered Rouen on August 30. Symbolically, on September 1, the *2nd Can. Div.* received the honour of liberating Dieppe. After operations around Dunkirk, the autumn fighting on the Albert canal and at the mouth of the river Scheldt was especially demanding. In February and March 1945, the *2nd Can. Div.* fought in Germany as far as the Rhine before finishing the war in the Netherlands.

The Swedish-designed 40 mm Bofors (shown here, the gun preserved at the Juno Beach Centre), formed the backbone of the Allied AA units, including the Americans. The Germans also used it (4 cm Flak 28). Photo T. Le Sant

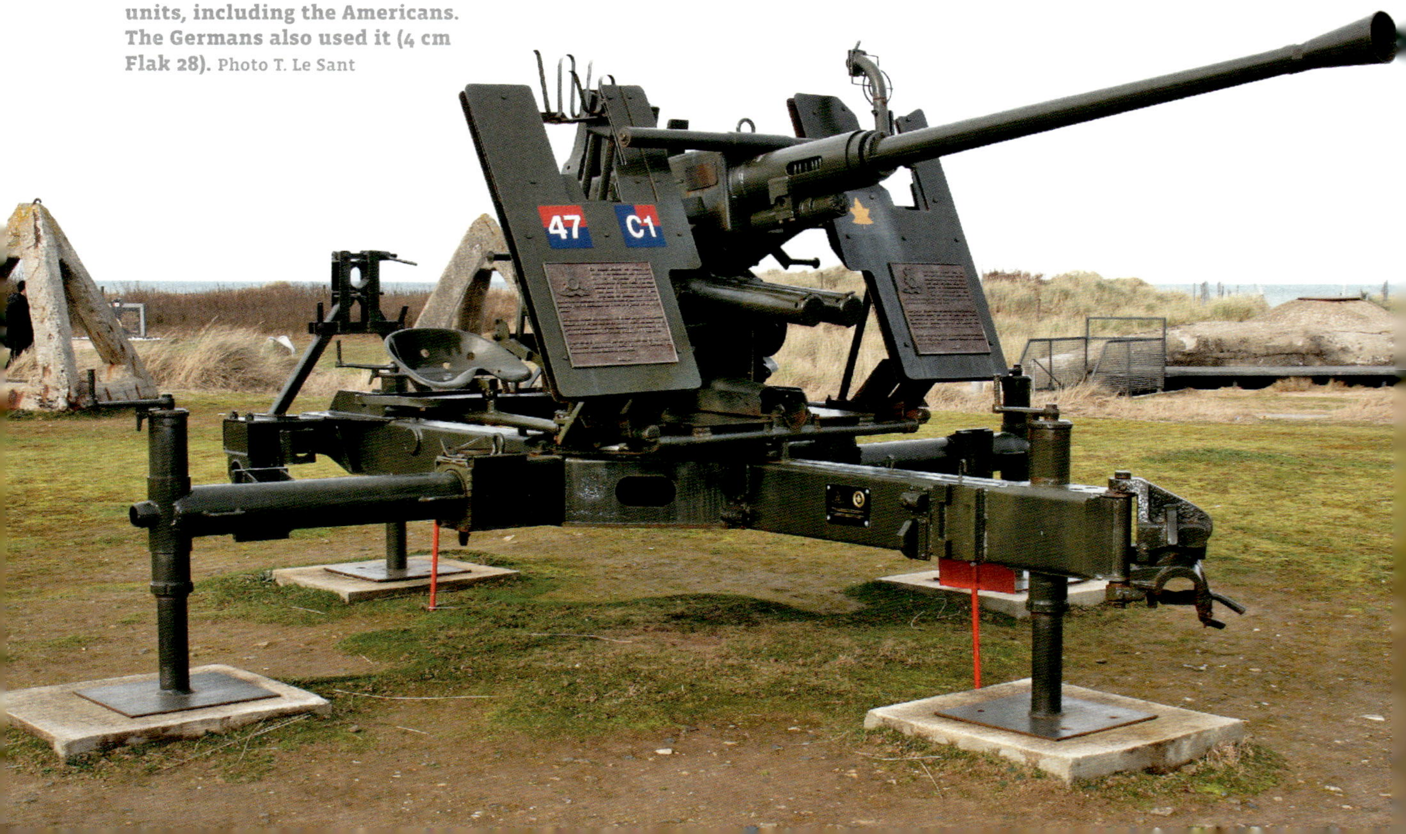

A much sought-after prize for Allied soldiers looking for souvenirs: a Nazi flag. Who knows if this one made its way back to Canada one day ... This excellent propaganda shot dates from August 10 1944. Soldiers Roy and Parker of the Queen's Own Cameron Highlanders of Canada had every reason to be pleased with themselves: their 2nd Canadian Division was on its way! By the end of *Operations Totalise* and *Tractable*, Falaise had fallen into their hands. PAC

90th US Infantry Division « Tough Ombres »

A GI in the uniform typical of summer 1944, topped with the famous M1 helmet which actually combined two helmets fitted together, one light and one heavy. At that time, the GIs did not wear 'rangers' but Combat Service boots with gaiters to protect them from water and mud.
Coll. T. Le Sant

The entwined T and O insignia of the 90th US ID refers to the geographical origin of the division's recruits. They were the men of the West, from Texas and Oklahoma.
Coll. T. Le Sant

The *90th ID* was ready to begin in Normandy on June 9, its first elements having landed on *Utah* on the 6. The initial fighting toward Pont-l'Abbé were costly from the very beginning. The division faced real difficulties during its first engagements, to such a point that Bradley asked himself whether it would not be preferable to dismantle the unit to reinforce other divisions. The idea was not carried out. In fact, the failures of the beginning of the campaign were blamed on the incompetence of the division's senior officers. From June 13 onwards, Bradley intervened by relieving the divisional commander, Brigadier-General McKelvie, of his command. This man, answering to the nickname 'Oral Null' was certainly not up to the job. Cold, and not paying attention to advice, he also seemed to be unaware of infantry tactics.

As always, the artillery was one of the keys to the final success. However, it was difficult to locate the German positions, and the too-great proximity to the American lines did not always allow them to provide the expected support.
Coll. T. Le Sant

TAKING MONT CASTRE

Unusually violent fighting engulfed the sector from July 3 to 9, most often under a threatening sky. The *90th ID,* which lacked cohesion and experience, was poorly served by the dense network of hedgerows bordering narrow, bumpy paths. In spite of a considerable artillery and armoured personnel carrier support, over the first days, the *358th and 357th IR* were severely tested on the southern flank of Mont Castre. On the eastern flank, the *359th IR* made better progress. On July 3, a single 88mm gun stopped the advance of the *358th IR* in its tracks, with only ten shells causing havoc in the American ranks. The fighting raged and the Germans were finally forced to concede the summit. On July 6, four American battalions took up a precarious position there. Two companies were surrounded and 250 men had to lay down their arms. However, the *90th ID* maintained its control of the important hill. On July 8, with 2,000 losses in five days for only 6 kilometres gained, it was exhausted.

From mid-June onwards, the division only held the role of a flank guard. It was not involved in the cutting-off of Cherbourg and did not participate in the reduction of the pocket around the great port At the end of June, its losses already amounted to 2,399 men, most of whom had fallen during the first week of the engagement. On July 3, a far more dangerous test awaited the *90th ID:* the fighting for Mont Castre, in the direction of La Haye-du-Puits. If it carried out its task laboriously, this terrible battle did not, however, end its commitment in the hell of the Hedgerows. By the end of July, its losses amounted to 6,994 men, or almost half of its initial strength. Major-General Landrum had not, however, convinced Bradley who decided to dismiss him, in his turn. Teddy Roosevelt was expected as commander of the division for a time, but he died of a heart attack. Bradley then decided to entrust the *90th ID* to Major-General MacLain.

GIs of the 357th IR in the La Madeleine sector at the beginning of June. The columns were advancing with caution: mines and other booby traps were a constant fear. The men are moving along the hedgerows, ready to take shelter at the slightest alert. Bad luck for the GIs of the 90th US ID: their officers were not up to their job ... NARA

The *bocage* was confusing: the field of vision was reduced, and the officers had the greatest difficulty in knowing precisely where their men were, and following the progress of neighboring units. Every hedge was fortified and, even with the support of armoured vehicles, it took courage to dare to cross an open field. NARA

The baptism of fire for the 90th US ID in the Cotentin *bocage* was disastrous: losses were heavy and, on June 13, Bradley was compelled to dismiss MacKelvie, its commander. NARA

On August 1, during the operational phase of *Cobra*, it liberated Saint-Hilaire-du-Harcouët, then headed for Le Mans. It then played a major role in the final phase of the battle of Normandy by participating effectively in the final closing operations around the Falaise pocket. It pushed back the counter-attacks of the *2.SS and 116.Panzerdivisionen* with style, in the Bourg-Saint-Léonard sector. The *Tough Ombres* continued their progress north and met up with the Poles of the *1st Polish Arm. Div.* at Chambois on August 19. The position was still poorly secured, and the Americans achieved a great success. On August 22, the battle was over and the sound of weapons ceased in the hell of the Poche. The *90th ID,* now experienced, claimed the capture of 12,000 enemy soldiers.

In autumn 1944, the hard struggles of Lorraine and the Sarre took place before they took part in Patton's counter-attack on the southern flank of the German armies engaged in the Ardennes. The *90th US ID* then participated in the German campaign and was in Czechoslovakia when the Germans surrendered.

17.SS Panzergrenadier-Division « Götz von Berlichingen »

This Panzergreandier of the Götz von Berlichingen is wearing camouflage trousers and a multi-coloured jacket, a Tarnjacke. The Waffen SS had the advantage of a good supply of camouflage garments, sometimes reversible (summer/autumn), in different models and with different patterns. Coll. T. Le Sant

Raised in November 1943, this division, commanded by SS-Brigadeführer Ostendorff and then SS-Standarda-rtenführer Baum, did not constitute an *SS* elite division, by failing to be fully operational. The division certainly included 17,321 soldiers but it lacked 1,700 - nearly 40% - of its officers. If the division had almost 1,400 cars and motorcycles, the number of lorries and tractors available on May 15 1944 was very low for a motorized division, as there were only 257 out of a theoretical supply of 1,686. On the other hand, its weaponry was not lacking, with 42 *Sturmgeschützen*, 12 *Marder IIIs*, 155 guns (artillery, *Pak* and *Flak*), 99 mortars and 1,008 *MG 34-42s.*

The insignia of the 17. SS Panzergrenadier-Division,Götz von Berlichingen'.

DEFENDING SAINTENY

At the beginning of July 1944, the *17.SS* had blockaded the sector stretching from Carentan to Sainteny. On the 4th, it faced the shock of the assault of the inexperienced *83rd US ID*. 150 *SS* fell, as against 400 Americans; the Americans also lost more than 1,000 men against Heydte's *Fallschirmjäger*, comrades in the struggle of the *Götz von Berlichingen* for nearly three weeks. The death toll of several days of fierce fighting, however, was very heavy for the *SS*. If they did not hesitate to carry out daring counter-attacks, their losses, particularly among the officers, were serious. A battalion commander, being held accountable for its appalling losses, even went so far as to prefer suicide to a court martial. On July 6, a daring *coup de main*, successfully undertaken by fifty men and four of Unterleutnant Hoffmann's *Sturmgeschützen* against a bridge located 10 kilometres inside American lines, did not change anything. On July 9, Collins' *7th US Corps* finally seized Sainteny. He had lost 5,000 men and progressed only 6 kilometres. On July 10, the *17.SS*, bled white, had no more than 1,000 infantry left.

A few Panzergrenadiere perched on a Sturmgeschutz ; a common practice, but highly dangerous because the infantry soldiers were very exposed. Coll. P. Tiquet

A self-propelled Flak 17. SS Panzergrenadier-Division . The unit had to advance to the front, suffering Allied air attacks: a foretaste for the SS of the absolute supremacy of the RAF and USAAF in the Normandy sky. Coll. P. Tiquet

The division, in position in the Vendée, handicapped by its lack of vehicles, began to move on June 7. The tanks are loaded aboard trains, while some units had to reach the front by bicycle. From June 8, the reconnaissance battalion was at Balleroy, offering a semblance of continuity on the Front despite an enormous gap in front of *Omaha*, of which the Americans were not aware. June 13 marked the division's first serious engagement, the counter-attack on Carentan, which had been abandoned by Heydte's *Fallschirmjäger*. Strongly repulsed by the paratroopers and American tanks, the *SS* lost 500 men. On this occasion, an episode perfectly reflected the fanaticism which governed the *Waffen SS:* an officer of the division, a veteran of *Das Reich*, shot down his own soldiers fleeing from the American armoured cars. By June 24, their losses had risen to 906 men.

The *Götz von Berlichingen* fought with a degree of effectiveness in the Taute sector, and inflicted significant losses on the *GIs* in their progress towards Sainteny. However, on July 23, the German High Command judged the division to be seriously weakened. *Operation Cobra*, which began two days later, caused further significant losses since the unit was partly surrounded in the pocket of Roncey. While the rear echelons were removed from the Front, one *Kampfgruppe* remained in action, and took part in the Mortain counter-attack, then in the desperate fighting of the Falaise pocket. Further south, in the Laval sector, two companies of the *SS-Panzerjäger-Abteilung 37* and its 31 *Jagdpanzers*, shipped from Germany, tried unsuccessfully to halt the American advance, before being driven back in their turn. The total losses in the West during the summer of 1944 amounted to 8,000 men.

The battle of Normandy was still not the final confrontation for this unit. In September 1944, it took part in the desperate fighting for Metz, in Lorraine, before being involved in *Operation Nordwind*, launched on the Alsace in January 1945. Driven back to Bavaria in the spring of 1945, the division fought its last battles there.

Two GIs looking at the body of a German soldier, huddled over the barrel of a Sturmgeschutz III. The discreetly marked dimensions of the tank are clearly visible on this image. The 17. SS had 42 of these devices.
Coll. T. Le Sant

3.Fallschirmjäger-Division

The 3. FJD was a well-trained division. All the Fallschirmjäger had followed a parachute training course. This one is wearing a camouflage jump jacket, model 42 (here with irregular patterns) over his smock. Clearly behind the front lines, he has fastened his helmet to his belt and is wearing a Feldmütze.
Coll. T. Le Sant

The *3. Fallschirmjäger-Division* was formed in Champagne in autumn 1943. The young volunteers, aged 21-22, had been trained specifically to fight against paratroops. The transfer to Brittany caused some delay with organisation and supply difficulties, especially as the equipment was late in arriving. The sparsely-populated Monts d'Arrée area, on the other hand, lent itself remarkably well to training. In order to strengthen morale within the division, the whole unit undertook parachute training.

In June 1944, Generalleutnant Schimpf's 17,420 men, full of confidence, were fully trained and prepared for battle. If the stock of ammunition was satisfactory, it still lacked part of its heavy weapons quota. The division had only 13 *Pak 40s;* apart from that, it had only one of its three artillery battalions, being twelve 105mm guns and nine recoil-less guns of the same calibre. The division's poor mobility was also a matter of concern, because barely 40% of the necessary equipment was available, spare parts were lacking and fuel supplies were insufficient.

The order to join the Front was received shortly after the Landings and, on June 12, most of the division was in position in front of Saint-Lô. The *Fallschirmjäger* put up a stubborn defence against the Americans. Lacking neither spirit nor courage, the paratroops took advantage of the *bocage* terrain, which was particularly favourable to the defenders. The fanaticism of the young *Fallschirmjäger* was as strong as that of the *Waffen SS*, and they made formidable adversaries.

After a month and a half of struggle in front of Saint-Lô, the paratroops, forced to fall back after *Cobra*, still put

The insignia of he 3.Fallschirmjäger-Division

The German paras lacked vehicles, which was a handicap when advancing to the Front in Normandy. Furthermore, the intense enemy air activity forced them to post spotters on each vehicle, which in addition had to be covered with branches to complete their camouflage and concealment.
Coll. P. Tiquet

The Fallschirmjäger were the elite soldiers. Their training and their characteristic uniform reinforced this feeling of team spirit. The bare-headed para has an MP 40 magazine carrier, the weapon which is held by the other officer, seen in profile. The man in the middle seems to be carrying a bag of grenades over his shoulder. On the left, the young para has been supplied with a fearsome MG 42 machine-gun. They all look determined, but their features are also marked by the bitterness of the combat. Bundesarchiv

up a tenacious resistance outside Vire. On July 26, the second day of the United States offensive, the *5th US Corps* recorded the loss of 980 men for a gain of just two kilometres. 283 *Fallschirmjäger*, belonging to seven different battalions, were captured that day. Shut into the trap of the Falaise pocket, the division managed to break out through the Polish curtain with more than 2,000 soldiers. The *Fallschirmjäger* were among the Poles most resolute opponents, determined to cross the obstacle of Mont Ormel and to open up a way for the other encircled units.

LAST FIGHTING OUTSIDE SAINT-LÔ

Faced with the *29th US ID* on the Martinville ridge, or the *2nd US ID* on Hill192, the paratroops held every hedge and every winding lane until the bitter end. Their overhanging positions, their infiltrations and their audacious counter-attacks caused the *GIs* considerable problems. On July 11, the *FJR 9* launched a night counter-attack. After an artillery bombardment, 250 *Fallschirmjäger* wove their way through the breaches. The surprise effect, however, was not enough to beat the *1/115th US IR*. The same day, *GIs* of the *2nd US ID* attacked Hill 192 once again. Despite a bombardment by 25,000 shells at the beginning of the assault, the quality of the defences was such that the Americans had to fight a desperate battle to seize it. Major Bingham's *2/116th US IR* was cut off for a time, but American control of the heights made it impossible for the Germans to remain in Saint-Lô, which was reached on July 18. The losses were, however, high in the ranks of the *Fallschirmjäger*, for they had reached 4,064 men by mid-July.

A Zündapp KS750 and its two passengers, two Fallschirmjäger, apparently from the medical corps if we judge by the flag displayed on the side-car as well as by the armband on the driver's left arm. This does not stop the latter from carrying, at his back, a pistol in its holster on his belt. Coll. P. Tiquet

The division was virtually destroyed in Normandy and during its retreat, especially in the Mons pocket. By September 4, the losses of the division and the formations to which it had been attached amounted to 26,179 men, of whom 2,561 had been killed. It commits Becker's *Kampfgruppe* to action during the battle of Arnhem. Back in action during the counter-offensive in the Ardennes, it was by then only a shadow of the excellent unit which had fought in the summer of 1944. The new recruits showed neither the fighting spirit nor the professionalism of their predecessors in Normandy. It finally disappeared in the *Kessel* blaze in the Ruhr in April 1945.

The Volkswagen Type 82, known as the Kübelwagen. The first model was delivered in 1939. With a range of 380 km and able to reach 80 km/h, 55,000 models were manufactured. It was, to a certain extent, the German equivalent of the Jeep. Photo T. Le Sant

5.Fallschirmjäger-Division

This NCO from the 5.FJD is properly equipped for combat: MP40 submachine gun, side-arm and stick grenade. The belt and holster are brown leather, typical of the Luftwaffe, whose insignia can be seen on the belt buckle, painted in grey-blue. The man is carrying a cloth gas-mask on his chest, of a model specially designed for paratroops since the standard metal design was considered too dangerous to be carried when jumping. The helmet was daubed with camouflage paint, a practice which was common in Normandy.
Coll. T. Le Sant

Raised in March 1944, Generalleutnant Wilcke's *5.Fallschirmjäger-Division* was of much less combat value than the *3.FJD*. Like the *3.FJD*, the 5.FJD was billeted in Brittany, and the young recruits were trained by a handful of veterans. On May 22 1944, it had only 12,836 *Fallschirmjäger* - a shortfall of almost 5,000 men. The troops were insufficiently trained, and barely 10% of the men had ever made a parachute jump. This, however, can be put in perspective, as the soldiers were never

The Insignia of the 5.Fallschirmjäger-Division

This Fallschirmjäger, probably one of a team of machine-gunners judging by the cartridge belt, is wearing the typical para cartridge belt round his shoulders and fastened at the waist by a belt with a buckle decorated with the Luftwaffe eagle. His helmet has been daubed with camouflage paint, while his comrade has chosen a wide-mesh net.
Bundesarchiv.

actually required to carry out an operational jump. The equipment available was of equivalent standard. The division had barely 9% of its theoretical vehicles. The anti-tank battalion only had three *Pak 40s* in place of its theoretical 36, while a single artillery battalion, with eighteen guns, had been supplied. On the other hand, the *Flak* battalion did have its twelve 88mm *Flak* guns.

After the invasion, the paratroops moved forward in a very piecemeal way, some units not reaching the Front before July. For most, the journey was carried out on foot, for almost 200 kilometres. On June 8, in a symbolic way, so as to ensure that the *5.FJD* reached the front, the *HQ* of the *VII. Army* requisitioned all available

MONT CASTRE

In spite of its appalling lack of preparedness, the *5.FJD* was able to show its teeth. Oberst Gröschke's *Fallschirmjäger-Regiment 15* fought tenaciously on Mont Castre. The mortars and *Nebelwerfer,* as well as bursts of machine gun fire, mowed the Americans down. Night attacks, infiltrations, cutting off the *bocage* terrain: the *Fallschirmjäger* turned everything to its advantage. On July 6, in bad weather, the *90th US ID GIs* managed to take the northern slopes of Mont Castre. The Americans of the *357th IR* penetrate the hamlet of Beaucoudray, but the paras hung on and dominated the opposing positions, especially from a supporting position in the ruins of a medieval castle. A *FJR 15* counter-attack isolated two American companies, with the help of another counter-attack, aimed at re-taking Le Plessis-Lastelle . The trapped *GIs* had no alternative other than to lay down their arms. Six men only just managed to return to the American lines. The Germans claimed the capture of 255 *GIs*. Before these defensive successes on Mont Castre, the general staff of the *VII. Army* hoped that the entry of the other *5.FJD* regiments into the fray would meet with as much success as that of the *FJR 15*. Its success, however, was costly. The *FJR 15* actually posted the loss of two-thirds of its 1,020 infantrymen.

The paras were soon exhausted by the fierce fighting on Mont Castre. The ranks were quickly thinned. They claimed, however, the capture of 859 GIs with their comrades of the 353. ID. Coll. Arromanches Militaria

This combat group is taking a few moments of rest in a farmyard. One of the paras is holding a shovel. They had to dig in, as soon as a position was reached. The paras had received orders to hide and only to open fire at very close quarters: 10 or 20 m. Coll. Arromanches Militaria

transport, including that belonging to the *Luftwaffe* and the *Kriegsmarine*. During this advance to the Front, while they were still in Brittany, a group of parachutists agreed to surrender to the FFI, who persuaded them that American armoured cars were in the vicinity. This episode says a lot about the reliability of these young recruits.

Its first battalion took up position on the Saint-Lô front on June 25. In fact, the different regiments of the division were attached to more seasoned units, and the *5.FJD* never fought as a single, composite group. On 11 July, the *II. Fallschirm-Korps* went so far as to claim that in its sector - toward Saint-Lô - it had despatched a regiment of *5.FJD* to strengthen the enfeebled *3.FJD*. This request was refused by the *VII. Army*, due to the difficult situation in which the *LXXXIV. Korps*, which was defending the area south of La Haye-du-Puits, found itself. As a baptism of fire, Count von Schulenburg's *Fallschirmjäger-Regiment 13* was liberally bombed by the Allied forces as they arrived at the front line. Equally inexperienced, the *Fallschirmjäger-Regiment 14* saw its officers expose themselves unnecessarily and unwisely: on July 17, it lost two-thirds of its officers in this way, during a single attack. *Operation Cobra* sounded the death knell of the division since two regiments out of three were wiped out - not without putting up a fierce fight - especially at Marigny. From then on, the last regiment and the support units still in the front line were attached to the *3.FJD*. After the fighting outside Vire and within the Falaise pocket, the losses were estimated at 8,000 men, leaving a strength of under 4,000 soldiers, of which few were infantrymen.

After its withdrawal, the *5.FJD* took part in the fighting in the Netherlands during *Operation Market Garden*. Reorganized and re-manned, it was engaged on the southern flank of the Ardennes counter-offensive. It fought on the Ardennes western flank until the end of the war. Part of the division was lost in the Rurh pocket in April 1945.

A Schwimmwagen Type 128, which is actually an amphibious Kübelwagen. The Fallschirmjäger had a certain number of them. The 5. FJD, however, had barely 9% of the vehicles with which it should have been supplied in theory ... Photo T. The Sant

2.SS Panzerdivision « Das Reich »

A motorcyclist of the 'Das Reich' on his DKW Nz 350. As at May 15, the division still only had 124 motorbikes out of its 1,895 theoretical supply. The unit had actually returned from the Eastern Front bled white, and had to replace its staff.
Coll. T. Le Sant

The *Das Reich* had been in all the campaigns since 1939, including the battles of Kharkov and Kursk in 1943. In June 1944, reorganized, the division was in reserve in the south-west of France. SS-Gruppenführer Lammerding had 17,283 men at his disposal on July 1, plus 39 *Panthers*, 78 *Panzer IVs* and 41 *Sturmgeschützen*, including 158 armoured cars. The division committed a total of 208 tanks and assault guns to the combat in the course of the campaign. Ready to move on June 7, it received the order to make for the Front on June 12. In the meantime, von Rundstedt assigned it to anti-partisan operations, which led to the massacre of civilians, notably at Oradour-sur-Glane and Tulle. The crimes continued in Normandy. On August 15, the *GIs* were filled with hatred after they discovered the body of the commander of the *708th Tank Battalion*, shot by the *SS* after his capture.

The lack of transport vehicles, plus Allied air activity, also caused difficulties in the units' movement up to the Front. On June 16, however, the motorised units assembled in the Mortain sector. The mechanised units transported by rail - especially the *Panzers* - had greater difficulties: on June 19, five trains ferrying *Panthers* were at Le Mans. Some units, however, did not leave the south-west of France until the end of July.

On arrival in the Périers sector, the division's units were engaged throughout various scattered *Kampfgruppen*. Lammerding was aware of the Allied superiority, but intended to turn his troops into

The insignia of the 2.SS Panzerdivision 'Das Reich'.

Marigny, July 29. This Sturmgeschütz has not withstood an aerial attack, which has reduced the neighbouring buildings to rubble; the machine has also lost its tracks. This armoured vehicle belonged to the 'Das Reich', which had 25 operational Sturmgeschütze on July 23. The three GIs belong to the 1st US ID. They are, from left to right, Philip Aaron, Jim Ritchie, Carmine Calvanico and Howard Strella. NARA

fanatics; he remained convinced that a superior fighting spirit would lead to victory for to him, Anglo-Saxon soldiers were inferior to German. By the end of June, the pressure exerted by the British toward the Odon forced Rommel to engage Weidinger's Kampfgruppe towards Noyers-Bocage. It suffered heavy losses - more than six hundred men - in the course of violent counter-attacks. Reinforced by fifteen 88mm *Pak* guns, the division was then sent north of Périers, in the American sector. It provided welcome support to the infantry units, which were trying to halt enemy progress beyond La Haye-du-Puits.

Launched on July 25, *Operation Cobra* threatened to surround the *2.SS Panzer*. Fighting proved particularly fierce at Marigny. On July 26, when Lammerding was replaced by SS-Standartenführer Tyschen, the Americans took Saint-Samson, 20 kilometres south of the positions held by the *SS*. Several columns led by *Panzers* managed to force a path through the enemy lines. On that occasion, July 27 and 28, Ernst Barkmann's *Panther* distinguished itself by burning no less than fifteen *Shermans*. If the losses in the Roncey pocket were sensitive, complete disaster was avoided within the division, then under the command of Otto Baum.

This division was in a position to participate in the Mortain counter-offensive, in the course of which it hardly covered itself with glory. Its inability to take Hill 314, on which an isolated American battalion was entrenched, constituted one of the major failures of the operation. Between August 13 and 18, 12,000 soldiers of the *Das Reich* withdrew from the Falaise pocket before it was closed. At the collecting point for units escaping from the trap towards Vimoutiers, the *Das Reich* put all its energies into covering the retreat of the remains of the *VII. Army*, and managed to cut the Poles off on the heights of Mont Ormel. It then covered the general retreat toward the Seine, before crossing the great river itself. With perhaps 7,000 losses, the division came out of the hell of the battle of Normandy with reasonable strength, but few *Panzers*. The only *Panzer* regiment had destroyed 200 Allied tanks.

Restored to condition, the *2.SS Panzer* took part in the Battle of the Bulge, particularly in the Manhay sector, before being transferred to the East for the offensive on Budapest. In May 1945, the division managed to escape capture by the Soviets by surrendering to the Americans.

Number of operational *Panzer* and *Panzerjäger*

June 1	102
July 1	112
July 23	103
August 21	15

COUNTER-ATTACKS TOWARDS SAINT-JEAN-DE-DAYE AND SAINTENY

On July 8, *Kampfgruppe* Wisliceny's counter-attack at Le Dézert and the intervention of units in the Sainteny sector brought about severe losses. The maze of hedgerow-lined paths did not facilitate the assailants' task. SS-Oscha Barkmann claimed his first *Sherman* that day. The counter-attack held out. Threatened with encirclement, the *Waffen SS* was forced to fall back. They abandoned five *Panzers* on the ground. In the Hommet Wood sector, of Hommet, a single company caused chaos in the ranks of the *9th US ID*. Some *Waffen SS* fanatics attacked while singing the patriotic song *"O Deutschland hoch in Ehren ". (Most honourable Germany)*. By July 10, the *Das Reich's* losses amounted to 1,221 men. At the same time, the *SS* claimed to have destroyed 128 American tanks by July 12.

2nd US Infantry Division « Indian Head »

An NCO of the 2nd US ID. He is armed with a Thompson sub-machine gun and a Colt 45 as well as a German handgun, a souvenir to take back to the United States, with a holster worn on a German belt, also captured.
Coll. T. Le Sant

Soldier of a wealthy army, the GI had the benefit of a smart dress uniform cut like a proper suit, like this officer of the 2nd US ID.
Coll. T. Le Sant

These American soldiers, perhaps in the 2nd US ID, interrogate three prisoners in the shelter of a hedge. A fourth German, wounded, is stretched out on the left. Gathering information on the ground meant the need to send out patrols and raids to bring in captives. Archives du Calvados

The insignia of the 2nd US ID 'Indian Head' Coll. T. Le Sant

The *2nd US ID* was one of the few *US Army* divisions of the period between the two World Wars. On June 7, the division, commanded by Major-General Robertson, was ready for action, in Normandy. It began at once, with the widening of the narrow Omaha bridgehead. The last few pockets of resistance in the vicinity of the beaches were cleared, and Trévières fell during the night of June 10. On the same day, the *2nd US ID* charged southwards and took control of the Cerisy forest. The strong opposition of the mauled remains of the German *352.ID* did not stop it from reaching Saint-Georges-d'Elle, but this first offensive now gave way to much more bitter fighting in the direction of Saint-Lô. Robertson still lost 855 men during this first week of combat. The spectre of the Hedgerow War awaited the *Indian Heads.* They remained blockaded for a month outside Saint-Lô and the terrifying Hill 192.

HILL 192

On July 11, after a month of a war of position, the *2nd US ID* finally seized the bloody Hill 192, east of Saint-Lô. The division lost 1,200 men at the foot of this hill, hotly defended by the entrenched German paratroopers on remarkably well camouflaged positions, which seemed impregnable. The strategic heights mocked the *Indian Heads* for a month. It took bloody hand-to-hand fighting, sometimes with bayonets and trenching tools, to remove the *Fallschirmjäger* from their position and repel their counter-attacks. The final assault was the result of careful artillery preparation, meticulously planned and carried out. It was, however, not sufficient to cause the collapse of the *Fallschirmjäger's* plan. At nightfall, after ten hours of fighting, the *1st Bn 38th US IR* had to give in, just three hundred metres from the top of Hill 192. Lacking munitions, exhausted, bombarded by their opponents and with significant losses, the *Fallschirmjäger* had to fall back to new positions on the axis of the Saint-Lô – Bérigny road. The *2nd US ID* had certainly not achieved all its objectives, but its determination and the sacrifices it made on Hill 192, undeniably played a key part in the taking of Saint-Lô.

American soldiers pass through the village of Colleville shortly after D-Day. The 2nd US ID landed on Omaha, but was not part of the first wave. It played an essential part in the taking of Saint-Lô, especially for its fighting on Hill 192. NARA

The *bocage* proved a formidable obstacle with its deep, winding paths and the hedgerows which divided up the landscape, channelling progression into a few narrow roads. The *GIs,* however, gradually became accustomed to *bocage* combat techniques. To protect themselves from snipers, for whom they were the favourite targets, the officers got into the habit of avoiding showing any insignia, as well as objects such as binoculars or map-cases. The Americans engaged 14 infantry divisions in Normandy. The fire-power of their German counterparts was, however, greater. On the other hand, the *US Army's* better supply of ammunition, as well as the effectiveness of its artillery, which was capable of providing considerable support, evened the odds. A 1944-type division of German infantry type would have had, in theory, 656 machine guns and 1,500 sub-machine guns. These last two figures would have been increased to 1,110 and 3,026 respectively in a division of German paratroopers. An *Infantry Division* like *Indian Head,* for example, would only have had 393 machine guns and 243 *Browning Automatic Rifles.* What is more, the latter were less efficient than the German weapons. On the other hand, there were many more infantry soldiers in a regiment of American infantry: 3,258 against 1,985, in theory, in a German infantry regiment. If the *2nd US ID* could benefit from the support of *Shermans* and *Tank Destroyers,* the German infantrymen were supported by excellent *Paks,* and had effective *Panzerfaüsten* and other *Panzerschrecks.* In addition, the *Panzers* could back up a defensive position.

GIs moving through the *bocage*. The soldier whose back view can be seen in the front row is carrying a mine detector, indispensable to detect the many traps laid by the enemy. On the right, the American armoured car is covered with foliage, a practice much more common in the opposite camp.
Archives du Calvados

Eisenhower came to check on troop morale: he is seen here in conversation with a sergeant of the 'Indian Head' at Cerisy-la-Forêt. If the 2nd US ID was not part of the first wave on D-Day, its road through Normandy was a long and bloody struggle in the maze of hedges. NARA

From July 29, after a brief rest, Robertson threw his men into *Cobra*, in the direction of Vire. They headed for Torigny-sur-Vire. The battle which took them to Vire was hotly contested, the Germans refusing to admit defeat. Furthermore, la Suisse Normande was a terrain which lent itself particularly well to the defence. On August 15, Tinchebray was liberated.

For the *2nd US ID*, the Battle of Normandy was over: Robertson received the order to make for Brittany. After the terrible fight for Brest, the *2nd US ID* was sent back towards the East. In December 1944, engaged toward the Roer, it was forced to halt his attack to counter the German offensive in the Ardennes. It crossed the Rhine in March 1945, seized Leipzig on April 18 and was in Czechoslovakia when Germany surrendered.

2nd US Armored Division « Hell on Wheels »

A soldier from the 2nd US Armored Division 'Hell on Wheels' wears a tank crewman's jacket as well as the overalls for men of that crew. The anti-shock helmet is also the model worn by tank crews.
Coll. T. Le Sant

Hell on Wheels was the *US Army's* first armoured division. It was raised in 1940 in the wake of the French disaster of that year, which showed the need for an armoured force. The man who took charge of the unit's training, before becoming its commander, was none other than George Smith Patton. The *2nd Arm. Div.* had the benefit of long, effective training before taking part in operations in North Africa and Sicily.

Following the example of the *3rd Arm. Div.* (also engaged in Normandy) and the *1st Arm. Div.*, which was subsequently reorganized, the *2nd Arm. Div.* was the 'heavy' type. The 'heavy' type armoured division had 14,620 men, 232 medium *Sherman* tanks, 158 light *Stuart* tanks, 3,630 vehicles and 54 self-propelled guns. If the *Armored Division* lacked offensive power, *US Army* battle orders assigned it, above all, to an operational role.

The first elements of Major-General Brooks' *Hell on Wheels* landed on *Omaha* on June 9. The *2nd Arm. Div.* was the first American armoured division on the continent. Its first significant battle took place on June 13 at Carentan, when it pushed back the German counter-attack. The division then took part in the Hedgerow War, an inappropriate role for a mobile unit which had been trained for operations.

The triangular insignia was common to all Armored Divisions. The 2 indicates the number of the division. Each colour represents a service: yellow for cavalry, blue for the infantry, red for artillery.
Coll. T. Le Sant

A column from the 8th US ID en route for Avranches, on July 31. The 2nd US Armored Division took a major role in the breakthrough consecutive to *Cobra*as flank-guard to the east, and then by closing the Roncey Pocket. The penetration of the enemy position by 'Hell on Wheels' was so rapid that the German general staff was not able to react quickly enough.
Archives du Calvados

THE RONCEY POCKET

On 29 July, *Hell on Wheels* proceeded to clear out the German forces who had been surrounded in the Roncey pocket. A column of the *Das Reich* was wiped out near Notre-Dame-de-Cenilly (17 killed and 150 wounded, for 50 American losses) and another was destroyed at Saint-Denis-du-Gast. The fighting remained fierce. A group of *Panzergrenadiere* of the *Das Reich* and *Götz von Berlichingen* divisions attacked the lines still held by the *2nd Arm.* in force, shortly before midnight on July 29, and in their passage swept away the *2nd Battalion, 41st Armored Infantry Regiment*'s command post. The unit commander, Lieutenant-Colonel Coleman, died - bazooka in hand - but not before destroying a *Panzer*. The breakthrough attempt was only stopped with the greatest difficulty. The scale of the disaster was revealed at daybreak: the Germans had suffered 130 dead, 124 wounded and 500 prisoners, as well as the destruction of seven *Panzers* and 25 armoured vehicles. The *GIs* had managed to withstand the shock, and only 100 were lost, with 12 vehicles destroyed. For their part, the self-propelled *M7 Priests* of the *78th Armored Field Artillery Battalion,* supported by *M10 Tank Destroyers*, destroyed a column of 11 armoured personnel carriers belonging to the *17.SS Panzergrenadier-Division*. The only *CCB,* which lost 395 men, including 42 were killed, claimed it had put 1,500 opponents out of action and captured 5,200 other Germans, as well as destroying 331 vehicles. A *Medal of Honor* and three *Distinguished Service Crosses* were awarded to the *GIs* of the *2nd Arm.* for the feats of weapons accomplished during these terrible night-long actions.

A 'Hell on Wheels' jeep, overloaded with equipment and armed with a .30 calibre (7.6 mm) Browning machine gun. The fast action and the speed of the 2nd US Armored Division columns destabilised the enemy: the breakthrough was finally made! Coll. T. Le Sant

On the other hand, the *2nd Arm. Div.* was successfully engaged in the course of *Operation Cobra*, launched on July 25. It was feared that the *bocage* would once again slow down progress. Many tanks - three fifths of them - were therefore fitted with the new hedge-cutter device invented by Sergeant Culin, and nearly 10,000 sappers were made available to the *7th US Corps* to lay out communications lines and repair the roads. The *Hell on Wheels* was also the first division to use the *Sherman Calliope*, filled with sixty-tube rocket launchers on the turrets. General Collins launched his armoured divisions on July 26. Charged with the protection of the breakthrough's eastern flank, Brooks assigned a more offensive mission to his division and forged through 12 kilometres, for light losses (three tanks, 200 men). Just like Collins, Pink, who commanded the division's *CCA*, understood that the Americans should not lose the initiative, and that speed of action and speed of progress were essential. When the staff learned that Rose had achieved its objective, namely a crossroads north of Mesnil-Herman, it seemed clear to everyone that the German front was finally breaking down, and that the long-awaited breakthrough had been achieved. Although most of its tanks had been equipped with a hedge-cutting device, the *2nd Arm. Div.* hardly had the chance to use Sergeant Culin's invention, since the American columns charged on the roads, rushing their opponent's defences with tactical air support.

Aware of the threat, von Choltitz hoped to be able to withdraw units of the left wing of the *LXXXIV. Korps* in time. On July 28, White's *CCB* thrust south of Coutances, towards Bréhal. Villebaudon and Lengronne were reached. The exit south was cut when he took control of the bridges on the Sienne. East of Coutances, the *3rd Arm. Div.* built a dam while the *4th* and *6th Arm. Divs.* were north of the town. A pocket was therefore forming at Roncey. The action carried out by the division during *Operation Cobra* can be regarded as the textbook realization of the doctrine for the use of armoured units within the *US Army* .

It's chow down time for Joseph de Freitos. This soldier has laid his rations out on the windowsill where he has placed his field stove to prepare a meal - no doubt monotonous, but welcome nonetheless. His multi-coloured camouflage uniform is more typical of the Pacific war. It was not much used in Europe, especially because it bore too close a resemblance to the Waffen SS camouflage uniform. NARA

Untersturmführer Peters of the III./ SS Panzergrenadier-Regiment 17 of the 'Götz von Berlichingen' is now a prisoner of war. Thousands of men, including many elite troops, were captured in the Roncey pocket, just like this Waffen SS soldier, or again like the para who can be seen behind the MP on the right, arms folded. NARA

Early in August, the division was in a defensive position to protect the bottleneck of Avranches, through which Patton's *3rd US Army* had to pass. At the end of the battle of the Falaise pocket, Brooks led his division to the east and crossed the Seine at Mantes.

On September 2, 1944, the first American unit to cross the Belgian border in the vicinity of Tournai - twelve hours before any other US Army group - was a patrol of the *82nd Reconnaissance Battalion*, the scout unit of *Hell on Wheels*. The division participated in the hard fighting of autumn 1944 on the German border before taking part in the Battle of the Bulge. It crossed the Rhine on March 27 1945 and was ordered to stop its progress on the Elbe on April 20. In July, it was the first American unit to enter Berlin.

A powerful Sherman M4 fitted with a 105 mm Howitzer. It is therefore not a combat tank, but one which would give fire support. There would be one device of this type per medium tank company, and three in the Assault Gun Platoon, making six per battalion. Coll. T. Le Sant

4th Armored Division « Breakthrough »

The *4th US Arm. Div.* was raised in 1941. Like the *5th* and *6th US Arm. Divs.* engaged in Normandy, it was a light armoured division supplied with, in theory, 10,937 men, 2,653 vehicles and 54 self-propelled guns. It operated around three *Combat Commands: CCA, CCB* and *CCR*. The number of tanks was less than in a 'heavy' division (three battalions as against six): 263 Tanks (168 *Sherman*, 86 *Stuart*) as compared with 368. The new units were smaller, but better balanced in terms of armoured vehicles/infantry. Its reconnaissance troops only accounted for one squadron, in place of a battalion.

After seven months of training in the United Kingdom, General 'Tiger Jack' Wood's *4th US Arm. Div.* arrived in France on July 13, but could only participate in skirmishes before the launch of *Cobra*. However, in assigning it to defensive tasks ad hoc, Middleton, head of the *8th US*

An officer of the 4th Armored Division 'Breakthrough' consulting a map before continuing the advance. A leather map holder hangs on his left, with a binocular case across his chest. He is armed with a pistol, and especially of an M1 rifle, a weapon which was not very powerful, but lightweight and highly manoeuvrable.
Coll. T. Le Sant

The Jeep was one of the symbols of the liberation. 639,245 came off the assembly lines in American factories. Each light armoured division had 451 of them, in theory.
Coll. T. Le Sant

Corps, allowed this novice division to toughen up before making it his spearhead. *Cobra* began on July 25. Wood came on to the scene on July 28. The *4th US Arm. Div.* then carried out a remarkable in-depth breakthrough. Wood seized the important road junction of Coutances, totally ruined, from July 28, thus contributing significantly to the formation of the Roncey pocket, within which the elite divisions of von Choltitz's *LXXXIV. Korps* von Choltitz were breaking up. On the 30th, the *4th US Arm. Div.* was at Avranches.

Armoured vehicles from the 4th Armored Division pass by, to the cheers of civilians, on the road leading from Périers to Coutances. Wood's speedy action was exactly as advocated by Patton: an American-style Blitzkrieg.
Archives du Calvados

The first American unit to enter Coutances was the 4th US ID, on July 28. Patton then unleashed Wood on Avranches. Even though the American army was entirely motorised, the GIs also had to travel on foot. The man on the left is a German prisoner. The noise of jackboots marching over the ground gave way to the softer sound of American boots as well as the much noisier roar of the columns of the liberators' vehicles. NARA

Wood had succeeded in making the breakthrough and could then penetrate into Brittany. He reached Rennes on August 3, bypassed the town and moved on towards Châteaubriant, which he liberated that evening. This momentum, typical of the cavalry, frustrated Wood, as he was disappointed not to be sent eastwards, on the flank of the German forces engaged in Normandy. Rather than surrounding the flank of the *VII. Army, the 4th US Arm. Div.* was sent to Vannes, then Lorient. When his superiors finally gave

On July 30, Dager's CCB entered Avranches without a fight. The following day, Bruce Clarke's CCA moved from Sélune to Pontaubault. The division had, in theory, 168 M4 Sherman like the one shown here, as well as 86 light M5 Stuart tanks. Photo T. Le Sant

The insignia of the 4th US Armored Division 'Breakthrough'. Coll. T. Le Sant

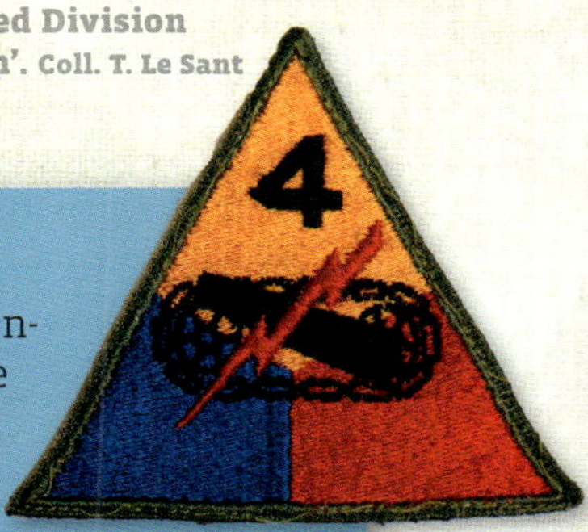

THE AVRANCHES BREAKTHROUGH

On the right flank of *Operation Cobra,* Patton oversaw the operations conducted by Middleton's *8th US Corps* before officially taking command of the *3rd US Army,* as soon as the American forces had reached Brittany. Fast and efficient, the *4th US Arm. Div.* had the honour of seizing the objective originally assigned to the *6th US Arm. Div. :* Avranches. On July 30, a column of the division, blocked by the destruction of the bridges over the Sienne, suffered losses in an ambush. The other column only just failed to capture Hausser, who was forced to flee on foot *in extremis.* On the evening of July 30, Dager's *CCB,* the vanguard of the *4th US Arm. Div.,* entered Avranches without a fight. What was more, a bridge over the Sée was secured. The German units retreating from the north ran into the *4th US Arm. Div.,* but, above all, tried to escape by skirting the obstacle. Furious fighting then took place at Avranches during the night of July 30. The following day, taking advantage of the chaos within the German defence, Bruce Clarke's *CCA* seized a bridge over the River Sélune at Pontaubault, in the course of the afternoon. Clarke had travelled 87 miles in four days, a real feat when one thinks of the slow progress made through the *bocage* since D-Day. Speed was gained by skirting obstacles and sowing chaos by keeping the columns on the move, while opening fire on all the supposed German defensive positions. Some officers even went so far as to spray every hedge with bursts of gunfire, just in case ...

him free rein, he rushed eastwards. The spearhead of Patton's army, his division distinguished itself during the fighting in Lorraine. In December 1944, it was the *Breakthrough*, then commanded by Hugh Gaffey (Wood had been relieved of his command for insubordination), Patton's favourite division, which raised the siege of Bastogne. After the passage of the Rhine in March 1945, still in the van of the *3rd US Army,* the *4th US Arm. Div.* crossed into Czechoslovakia on May 6, 1945. The unit had built a formidable reputation in Europe within the *3rd US Army.* Referring to the leader of their army, Lieutenant General George Smith Patton, Wood's soldiers nicknamed themselves *'Georgie's Boys'.*

The 4th US Armored Division's ride to Avranches on July 30 has become part of the legend of the battle of Normandy. The Norman civilians cheered their liberators as they passed by, as here in Bréhal. Mémorial de Caen

2.Panzerdivision

This machine-gunner is still equipped with an MG 34, a very effective weapon, but more expensive to produce than the MG 42. Not all Panzergreandiere had multi-coloured smocks: this one has also covered his canvas tent, to camouflage it. Coll. T. Le Sant

Recruited in Austria, this unit had taken part in almost all the *Wehrmacht's* campaigns: Poland in 1939, France in 1940, the Balkans in 1941, then the Soviet Union. Retired from the Eastern front during the winter of 1944, the *2.Panzer* was transferred to France, near Amiens, where it was restored to condition. Commanded by Generalleutnant von Lüttwitz, it was one of the cornerstones of the *Panzergruppe West.* Its training

The trident: the divisional insignia of the 2. Panzer-Division.
Photo T. Le Sant

An Opel-Blitz lorry meets a Panzer IV. It was risky to travel by day. The vehicles were therefore covered with branches, and took advantage of the most lightly wooded areas to hide under the trees. The Panzers were not spared by the USAAF's Jabos: a damaged machine, or one in the course of refuelling, could block an entire column ... Coll. P. Tiquet

TESSY-SUR-VIRE: BLOCKING *COBRA*

On July 28, the counter-attack of the *2.Panzer*, attached to von Funck's *XLVII. Panzerkorps*, caused significant American losses. The advance of the *19th US Corps* ran violently against the German *Panzers*. The *30th US ID's* manoeuvres, however - which provoked a counter-order from Hausser, the *VII. Army* commander - delayed the German armoured division's implementation. The confrontation, which took place at Tessy-sur-Vire, was the most difficult battle fought by the *GIs* after the launch of *Cobra*. At La Denisière, between Villebaudon and Le Mesnil-Herman, twenty-five *Shermans* were destroyed by a *Kampfgruppe*, which itself succumbed itself on July 30. The Germans actually threatened the American lines of communication, forcing them on to the defensive. The *743rd Tank Battalion* was reduced to thirteen appliances, as against the theoretical fifty-four *Shermans*. However, the *bocage* and the power of the American formations got the better of the German counter-attacks. Although first the intervention of the *2.Panzer*, then the *116.Panzer*, limited the American forces' progress, they did not have the resources to fill the breach and stabilise the Front. *Operation Cobra* was, therefore, a success: the German front in Normandy was crushed.

was smoothly carried out, and the new recruits had the time to take enough exercises to be prepared to repel the Allied invasion. It was, therefore, a division in excellent condition. Well trained, its 15,900 men were supported by 196 *Panzers*: 96 *Panzer IVs*, 79 *Panther*s and 21 *Jagdpanzer IVs.* The *Panzergrenadiere* were particularly well supplied with half-tracked *Sdkfz 251s*, as there were 476 in service within the two regiments. The anti-tank force was supplemented by 25 *Pak 40s* and 88mm *Flak*; the supply of artillery pieces, moreover, was complete.

The alert was given on the night of June 8 - 9, and the motorised columns set off in the rain - a journey which was not without effect on their engines - and crossed the Seine in Paris. The *Panzers* made part of the journey by train, and the *Panthers* did not reach the front until June 19: the first units arriving at the Front had to confront the Allies without the support of armoured vehicles. The units in the vanguard were in position between Villers-Bocage and Caumont on June 12. This area made up the combat sector assigned to the division for the entire month of June. The *2.Panzer* filled the gap caused by the collapse of the *352.ID* after the fighting on *Omaha Beach*.

The struggle in the *bocage* against the Americans, was hard-fought, and Lüttwitz managed to contain his opponents. At the end of June, a *Kampfgruppe* organised around the *Panther* battalion took part in the fighting of *Operation Epsom*. This *Kampfgruppe* proved fatally effective, since it claimed the destruction of 53 British tanks and 15 anti-tankguns on a single day, June 28. In that way, the *Panzers* showed their superiority. By July 1, the *Panther* battalion had destroyed 89 tanks, 19 anti-tank and 13 light-tracked armoured vehicles, only losing 20 *Panzers* itself. The losses in men during June amounted to 1,201 soldiers.

They had to wait until July 21 for the division be relieved by the *326.ID*. The relief was barely carried out before the American breakthrough which followed *Cobra* forced von Kluge to throw the *2.Panzer* against the American's flank. The German counter-attack did not lack spirit, but could do nothing to change the course of events:

The 2. Panzer-Division was well equipped with Sdkfz 251, since its two Panzergrenadiere regiments had 476. The device provided mobility and protection for the Panzer's indispensable companions.
Photo T. Le Sant

On the left, Major Curry, gun in hand, has just achieved his objective: his Canadian Shermans had taken Saint-Lambert-sur-Dive and closed off an exit route for the Germans. The casualty list was 800 killed and wounded and 2,100 prisoners, including Hauptmann Rauch, seen here in the centre of the photograph. PAC

Lüttwitz was now threatened from the rear by *Operation Bluecoat* and the *2.Panzer* had to be redeployed in the south, in view of *Operation Lüttich,* launched towards Mortain. With 2,220 soldiers and 75 *Panzers*, the *2.Panzer* still represented a formidable force, and formed the spearhead of their last counter-offensive. Lüttwitz decided to surprise the opponent by attacking without artillery preparation. The *2.Panzer* managed to reach Le Mesnil-Adelée, but the few successes it achieved had no future.

Retired from the front because of the threat of the *15th US Corps,* which had reached Le Mans, on August 13, the division regrouped in the forest of Écouves. Saving most of its service units, the *2.Panzer* managed to escape from the Falaise pocket on August 19, before it was closed. Between August 21 and 23, it re-grouped in the Bernay area. When it crossed the Seine, it only managed to save five *Panzers*. The division's losses during the campaign were estimated at about 7,000 men.

It was re-formed, and took part in the Battle of the Bulge in December 1944, in the Bastogne sector. It was the unit which had advanced the farthest west in the course of the offensive, falling a few kilometres from the Meuse. According to the Americans, the *2.Panzer* was one of the best German units they faced during the campaign to liberate north-west Europe. In the spring of 1945, they surrendered in Plauen and Kœtzing..

Number of operational *Panzer* and *Panzerjäger*

May 31	177
July 1	118
August 6	75
August 11	22

654.Schweres Panzerjäger-Abteilung

Commanded by Hauptmann Noak, this battalion of heavy tank destroyers was the first unit to use *Jagdpanthers* - or even *Jagdpanzer V, Sdkfz 173s* - against the Allies. These machines, of which there were twenty-five, were formidable opponents of the Allied tanks. Armed with a redoubtable 88mm L/71 gun - like the *Königstiger* - , these tank destroyers, which were mounted on a *Panther* chassis, were formidably armoured: the armour plating of the casemate could be as much as 100 mm.

The battalion was originally placed on the line at Valognes, but when Cherbourg was cut off, the German high command was forced to reassign the unit to another sector. The unit was then assigned to the *Panzer Lehr* sector, and was finally committed beside the infantry formations. On the front line since

These tank crew members of the Schwere Wörter - Panzerjäger-Abteilung 654 wear double-breasted field grey uniforms, characteristic of Sturmgeschütze crews. The braid on the collar tabs and shoulders are red, not pink: the assault guns, the Sturmartillerie, were attached to the artillery and not to the armoured car division, to Guderian's great annoyance. Coll. T. Le Sant

British armoured vehicles in Saint-Martin-des-Besaces. The *Bluecoat* offensive launched by Montgomery was faced with many Panzer units rounded up by Kluge, including the Jagdpanther of Schwere Wörter - Panzerjäger-Abteilung 654. DR

mid-July, its scores remained modest at first, with six British tanks destroyed between July 17 and 30. The *Jagdpanthers* supported the *326.ID* but were too few in number to halt the power of *Operation Bluecoat* alone. Noak had divided his armoured vehicles between four *Kampfgruppen*, two being first placed in the *326.ID's* sector and the other two in that of the *276.ID*. Nevertheless, the *Jagdpanthers* carried out a disastrous counter-attack on the British on July 31. By August 14, the total losses inflicted on the Allied armoured forces were confined to forty-two tanks, a total which seemed rather poor, given the excellence of the *Jagdpanthers.* It should be emphasized, however, that the fragile engines of these devices meant that operational vehicles very rarely exceeded 50 %.

If this great tank destroyer only obtained a moderate score against Allied armoured vehicles in Normandy, it did, on the other hand, provide an effective supporting role to the German infantrymen of *276.* and *326.ID.* On August 14, although there were still twenty *Jagdpanthers* on the strength, only two were capable of operating on the Front, because of the lack of spare parts. Under those conditions, on August 15, the battalion received the order to fall back to the Seine. Eleven armoured vehicles had to be sabotaged in the course of the retreat.

The Jagdpanther was the most effective, and the most redoubtable, tank hunter of the entire war. Just like the Tiger II, the Königstiger, it made its first kills in Normandy. The two machines photographed here are at Bourgthéroulde. But their weight constituted a handicap: could they cross the obstacle of the Seine? DR

LES LOGES, JULY 31: THE JAGDPANTHER'S FIRST COUNTER-ATTACK

On the second day of *Operation Bluecoat,* nineteen *Jagdpanthers* were in support of the *326. ID:* four were operational at *Kampfgruppe* Lüders, five others were available at *Kampfgruppe* Zwchenderlein, and ten tank destroyers were on reserve within*Kampfgruppe* Wittmoser. However, the day's feat was the work of only two of them.

The *Scots Guards (6th Tank Brigade)'s Churchill* tanks had reached the Loges ridge, between Caumont and Saint-Martin-des-Besaces. Oberleutnant Zwchenderlein - the commander of the *3/s. Panzerjäger-Abteilung 654* - decided to intervene by committing two of the five *Jagdpanthers* in his *Kampfgruppe*. Slipping through the *bocage*, the German armoured cars surprised enemy tanks, on which infantrymen, were casually perching At a distance of barely 300 metres, the piercing shells of the *Jagdpanther* and their machine guns sowed death and chaos. Thirteen *Churchills* were destroyed. It seemed that this success caused the loss of only one *Jagdpanther*, sabotaged by its crew, who had no breakdown repair equipment

11th British Armoured Division « Taurus Pursuant »

This tank crewman wears a sleeveless leather jerkin, showing a blue and white armband.
Coll. T. Le Sant

The *11th Arm. Div.*, trained by Major-General Hobart, one of the doyens of armoured vehicles across the Channel, had benefited from two and a half years of intensive training, which bore fruit. If the *11th Arm. Div.* was still inexperienced, it had in its ranks, however, an armoured regiment which had participated in numerous campaigns, and which had a competent staff. In addition, Major-General Roberts, who commanded the division, was a talented officer.

The bull painted on the side of this Cromwell tank shows unequivocally that it belongs to the 11th Armoured Division, a unit led by the masterly hand of General Roberts, an imaginative and rather independent-minded officer. The Cromwell was not supplied to the division's armoured brigade, but was part of its reconnaissance cavalry division. IWM

The start of their operations, in the context of *Epsom*, seemed promising. Engaged from June 27 in the narrow bridgehead won by the *15th Scottish Div.* , the *11th Arm. Div.* faced the elite of the *Panzer* units -*Tiger* and *II. SS Panzerkorps* - and suffered heavy losses in the fierce fighting which took place around Hill 112. Several dozen tanks and two hundred and fifty human lives were lost for insignificant results. The respite was, however, of short duration.

It was the *11th Arm. Div.* that Monty selected as the spearhead of *Operation Goodwood*, triggered from the bridgehead to the east of the Orne, in the hope of crushing the enemy front and reaching Falaise. The deployment and the entry of the division suffered, however, from the incredible congestion in the channels of communication crossing the Orne river and its canal. Roberts was appalled by the ambitious scale of the operation. He was also horrified at the lack of infantry support available to its armoured vehicle squadrons, which spear-headed the offensive. The hard fighting carried out beyond the Caen - Vimont railway line as far the Bourguébus sector drained the division's resources, in spite of an excellent final success won at Bras and Hubert-Folie against the *1.SS Panzerdivision's* defence. The advance of a dozen kilometres within the enemy's well-staffed and skilfully designed defences was not carried out without significant losses. The balance sheet was heavy, costing 191 tanks and 735 men.

This tank crewman of the 11th Armoured Division wears the black beret of the Royal Tank Regiment formations with the badge of the Royal Armoured Corps, which brought together the various armoured formations: first the Royal Tank Regiment and the cavalry units, then the reconnaissance units. Coll. T. Le Sant

The insignia of the 11th Armoured Division: 'Taurus Pursuant'.
Coll. T. Le Sant

A long-awaited moment for these Tommies of the 'Taurus Pursuant': the distribution of mail. At last, news from home! For others, these moments of respite were for reading a newspaper or, quite simply, just taking it easy. Individual foxholes had been dug in case of artillery fire but, on this flat ground, they did not seem to fear the Luftwaffe. This scene took place near Éterville and Baron, in the course of *Operation Epsom*. IWM

A Sherman of the 11th Armoured Division on June 11 1944. The sign in the rather precarious position on the left shows the direction of Paris and Berlin: the road to travel was still long, however, and many tank crews were lost to attacks from Panzers and Paks ... There is quite a diverse range of headgear to be seen: the tank crew helmet, the black beret of the Royal Tank Regiment and the classic British Mk II helmet. IWM

The injection of new equipment, combined with the dissolution of the anti-aircraft regiments to provide new tank crews, allowed these losses to be partially made up. The division distinguished itself once more with its offensive capabilities during *Operation Bluecoat*. Roberts' armoured division was once again placed in the first ranks, since it was an integral part of the *8th Corps*, which led the principle assault of the offensive. On that occasion, Roberts' innovation of organising his division around a mixed infantry-tank grouping proved genuinely effective so far as inter-weapon co-operation - not then the norm within the British forces - was concerned. The offensive began on July 31. The *11th Armoured* barely moved: mines, German tank counter-attacks and the terrain - *bocage* and hills - slowed it down. Within a few days, nearly eighty armoured personnel carriers were out of action. Vire was only 3 kilometres away, but the town had been transferred to the American sector.

LE PONT DU TAUREAU

The start of *Operation Bluecoat* was difficult for the *11th Armoured Division,* especially for the infantry, who suffered the accurate enemy fire. Nevertheless, on July 31, the *2nd Household Cavalry* charged the enemy lines. The reconnaissance unit carried off a considerable success by seizing intact a bridge on the Souleuvre, carelessly left unprotected by the enemy. By a lucky chance, the bridge in question was actually situated at the junction of the sectors held by the two front line German divisions, both believing that the other unit was defending the bridge. At first, Lieutenant Dickie Powle only had an armoured car and a scout-car. At 14:00, he was joined by the *4th King's Shropshire Infantry* and the *2nd Northampton Yeomanry.* Since then, the bridge has been known as Le Pont du Taureau (the Bridge of the Bull), in reference to insignia of the *11th Arm. Div.*

The fighting then intensified for the *11th Arm. Div.* and its losses rose when faced with *Panther* and *Tiger* counter-attacks. Fourteen tanks were set on fire by a single *Tiger* at Chênedollé. The operation cost a total of approximately two hundred men killed. Having to replace its men so as to return to operational strength as quickly as possible, the unit was boosted by the *Guards Arm. Div.* From August 14, the division was engaged in operations of first surrounding, then destroying the enemy in the Falaise pocket. Roberts' men fought towards Flers, Briouze, Putanges, Gacé - where the taking of the Touques bridge cost several tanks - and L'Aigle.

At the end of August, the Seine was crossed at Vernon and the unit marched on Amiens. On September 4, the *11th Arm. Div.* seized Antwerp. From October until December, it took part in the difficult clearing of the west bank of the Maas. In reserve when the Ardennes counter-offensive took place, Roberts' division was charged with the defence of the bridges on the Meuse in the Dinant and Namur sectors. Participating in the German campaign, the end of the war found them in Schleswig-Holstein, on the borders of the Reich and Denmark.

With the Comet, the 11th Armoured Division finally had a British-made tank to match the Panzers. But this tank only came into service at the end of the war.
Photo T. Le Sant

326.Infanterie-Division

This officer of the 326. ID has a camouflage jacket made out of tent canvas. The lamp attached to the chest pocket allowed the hands to remain free while still using the light. His personal armament includes a pistol and an MP 40 submachine gun, a weapon more often reserved for officers and NCOs.
Coll. T. Le Sant

The insignia of the 326. Infanterie Division.

The division, nicknamed *'Kriemhilde'* after the heroine of Norse legend, and commanded by Generalleutnant von Drabisch-Waechter, was raised in 1942. In the spring of 1944, it had not yet come under fire. It was in the process of being converted from a static unit to a 1944-type infantry division. It had 11,533 men, 10 *Sturmgeschützen* and 14 *Marder IIIs;* the number of tanks in *Panzerjäger-Abteilung 326* rose to 34 by early August. Nevertheless, the *326.ID* still lacked vehicles. Its artillery included many captured Soviet guns, a typical example of the disparate equipment with which a number of the infantry divisions guarding the *Atlantikwall* were supplied.

This photograph shows a Wehrmacht wagon and its harness It is a reminder that 80% of the German army still used horses in 1944: the infantry usually had to move on foot, while delivering supplies and pulling artillery pieces was carried out with horses. BnF

Securing the defence of the Atlantic Wall in the Pas-de-Calais, the *326.ID* was only engaged in Normandy from the end of the month of July. It relieved, in the Caumont-l'Éventé sector, the *2.Panzerdivision* which could then be sent to the west to halt the *Cobra* breakthrough. The division bore the brunt of the *Bluecoat* offensive. A major blunder was committed when the bridge, near La Forêt-l'Évêque, over the Souleuvre, was captured intact by the *11th Armoured Division*, left undefended since the *326.ID* thought this bridge was the responsibility of the paras on their left; and vice versa.

MONT PINÇON

Faced with the offensive of *Operation Bluecoat,* Mont Pinçon formed the key element of the German *Wehrmacht's* defensive system in la Suisse Normande, east of Vire. Reaching 365 metres and with steeply sloping sides, it seemed to constitute an impregnable stronghold. Losses were heavy and the *326.ID* could not continue to maintain its positions on Mont Pinçon. The Allies, however, had to pay a heavy price for victory. On August 6, the assault was jointly carried out by the *50th* and the *43rd ID.* The British fought through to the summit of Mont Pinçon, which they reached, exhausted by the strain of the combat and the climb. The first to arrive were the *Shermans* of the *13/18th Hussars (8th Armoured Brigade)* and a handful of infantrymen who had managed to overcome the obstacle, seemingly insurmountable, which the slope had represented. The storming of the top of the hill by seven armoured personnel carriers (one had toppled into the ravine and a ninth was destroyed by German anti-tank weapons) put an end to any further organized German resistance. The *Wiltshire Regiment* discovered trenches and no less than forty abandoned guns. At nightfall, the Mont Pinçon area was cleared.

Officers chatting in the grounds of a château. The man on the left wears an old-style cap dating back to 1934, prior to the creation of the German Wehrmacht. The 326. ID was hit hard by *Operation Bluecoat*, but the German infantry formations were tenacious and resilient. Coll. T. Le Sant

The *326.ID* was, however, deeply entrenched. Its system of defences was formed by strongholds such as the place known as les Sept Vents, on the road leading to Saint-Martin-des-Besaces. Certain positions, such as Hill 309, were key elements of its disposition. In fact, the mines, mortars and machine-guns of the *326.ID* and *Nebelwerfer* caused significant losses to the *11th Arm. Div.* attackers. Drabisch-Waechter did not hesitate to counter-attack, with the welcome support of the *Jagdpanther* of *Panzerjäger-Abteilung 654.* Despite the intervention of armoured troops, British pressure ultimately proved too strong for the *326.ID* and its neighbour, the *276.ID.* Drabisch-Waechter himself was killed; command then passed first to Oberst Kretsch and then to Oberst Kaschner.

Forced to retreat, the *326.ID* was surrounded in the cauldron of Falaise; a thousand men managed to escape, particularly on August 20, at Saint-Lambert. Its losses in the Campaign were at least 6,000 men.

The remnants of the division are used as the basis of a new unit, the *326.Volksgrenadier-Division*, implemented in Hungary in September 1944. Transferred to the Western Front, the *326.DGV* was engaged during the Battle of the Bulge. In April 1945, it disappeared into the furnace of the *Kessels* on the Ruhr, and in the Harz Mountains.

116.Panzerdivision

A tank crew member of the 116. Panzer in his black uniform. The grease stains do not show. The collar tabs bear the death's heads used by the armoured service, which caused confusion among the Allies who could easily mistake Panzer crewmen for the SS.
Coll. T. Le Sant

On D-Day, this division, raised in March 1944 from survivors of the Eastern Front, was located east of Rouen. In spite of its proximity to the Front of the invasion, it remained on reserve until the end of July. In fact, setting aside the threat of a major landing in the Pas-de-Calais or on the Somme estuary this large unit, controlled by Generalleutnant von Schwerin, was still far from being complete. Like the *Panzer Lehr*, the *116.Panzer* did not have its own *Panther* battalion. Instead, it had *Panthers* from the *I/ Panzer-Regiment 'Großdeutschland;* then those of the *I/ Panzer-Regiment 24* of the *24.Panzerdivision.*

The division had 86 *Panzer IVs*, and received 76 *Panthers* in June, then 21 *Jagdpanzer IVs* in July, too late to ensure adequate training for the crews. Including the 25 *Panzer IIIs, Sturmgeschützen, Panzerjägers* and short-barrelled 75 mm *Panzer IVs*, 209 armoured personnel carriers had served within the *116.Panzer* during the summer of 1944. The strength in terms of in men had risen to 14,358.

The greyhound, emblem of 116. Panzer-division. A Russian dog actually became the mascot of 16. Infanterie-Division, which formed the backbone of the armoured division.

A Panther is preparing to cross through the embankment of a hedge: a dangerous manoeuvre in the presence of the enemy - which was not the case here - because the machine then presented its less protected underside to hostile fire. The 76 Panthers of the 116. Panzer actually belonged to the 24. Panzer-Division, then in Russia.
Musée Mémorial de la Bataille de Normandie, Bayeux

On July 20 - the day of the failed attempt on Hitler - the *116.Panzer* finally crossed the Seine. Von Schwerin had claimed that Rommel had kept this unit back for political purposes, but this seemed rather dubious. The deployment and use of a *Panzer* division was first and foremost Hitler's responsibility.

On arrival in Normandy, *116.Panzer* was immediately faced with the American *Cobra* breakthrough. Its formations, still fresh, then counter-attacked the American right flank together with the *2.Panzer*. The project of an offensive on Saint-Lô was abandoned in favour of *Operation Lüttich*, the Mortain counter-attack. The counter-offensive held out because the *GIs* managed to arrest the *Panzer* division. When the problem of the Falaise pocket arose, the *116.Panzer* was deployed to the south-east to ward off the threat of the *15th US Corps*, who had captured first Le Mans,

OPERATION *LÜTTICH*

The *116.Panzer* took part, within the context of the *XLVII. Panzerkorps,* in the counter-offensive imposed by Hitler on his rather reluctant generals. It did not exactly shine. Schwerin, who disagreed with his commanding officer, Funck, delayed the deployment of his troops and refused to transfer a battalion of tanks to the *2.Panzer*. He was afraid that the *84.ID,* which was relieving his division and securing its right flank, was not sufficiently powerful to resist the American forces. The insubordinate Schwerin was temporarily replaced by Oberst Rheinard. On August 7, while *2.Panzer* was making some progress, the *116.Panzer,* which formed the right wing of the attacking front, to the north of the Sée, was not making any progress at all in the face of the American defenders. It had only committed three of its six *Panzer* columns: a fourth did not set off until five hours later. Before the tactical skill deployed by the *GIs* of the *39th IR,* with air support which seemed to be everywhere, the *116.Panzer,* blocked in the *bocage* of Mont Turgon, was unable to carry out its mission.

A Panzer IV of the Panzer Lehr, destroyed at Villers-Bocage on June 13. It was also near here that the 2.Panzer-Division engaged in one of their first fights in the Battle of Normandy. Private Collection.

then Alençon. They arrived in time to defend Argentan, crucial for the German retreat. The battle was fierce, but the *Panzer* division, although weakened and dependent on a rather erratic supply system, still managed to hold the town for several days, despite the pressure exerted by forces which were superior in number. This success formed a major contribution to the evacuation of thousands of soldiers, before the pocket was closed. Total losses in Normandy were 4,000 men.

In September 1944, pushed back to the German border, the *116.Panzer* took part in the fighting for Aix-la-Chapelle. In October, it gained a victory by wiping out the American troops who had captured the villages of Schmidt and Kommerscheidt, during the difficult and bloody battle of the forest of Hürtgen. Re-equipped, it became one of the spearheads of the *V. Panzerarmee* during the Battle of the Bulge. It was lost in April 1945 in the pocket of the Ruhr and the Harz Mountain range.

Number of operational *Panzer* and *Panzerjäger*

July 27	146
July 30	77
August 22	18

30th US Infantry Division

This American officer of the 30th US ID has collected a few souvenirs: a German officer's cap as well as a pair of binoculars. These were obviously useful, as was the German stick grenade slipped through his waistband.
Coll. T. Le Sant

The insignia of the 30th US ID 'Old Hickory'.
Coll. T. Le Sant

This division, raised in 1940, was an offshoot of the National Guard. On June 14, Major-General Hobbs embarked, with his *30th US ID*, for Normandy. His first engagement was to seize the heights dominating the Vire and the Taute. The division then took part in the bloody battle of Saint-Lô. On July 7, the *30th US* crossed the Vire in assault canoes and established a bridgehead at Saint-Jean-de-Daye, quickly consolidated by the engineers' putting several bridges into usable condition. The *30th US ID* was soon confronted with the most formidable enemy units engaged on the Western Front. Advancing toward Hill 91, les Hauts-Vents, which was bitterly disputed, it suffered the violent counter-attacks of the *2.SS Panzerdivision.* In the end, the *SS* nicknamed the dreaded *GIs* of the *120th US IR 'Roosevelt's SS Troops'.* On July 11, Hobbs was confronted by the *Panzer Lehr* in the vicinity of La Meauffe. Continuing its progress towards Pont-Hébert, which it seized with difficulty on July 14, it was once again faced with the elite of the enemy forces, in this case

The 30th US ID enters Évreux. The inspired defence by several Kampfgruppen had, however, held up the Americans, making the crossing of the Seine easier for several tens of thousands of men. NARA

the *Fallschirmjäger.* In just one week, its losses amounted to 3,200 men. The consumption of ammunition during the fighting in the *bocage* was much higher than had been originally anticipated. In some sectors, enemy artillery activity caused serious difficulties for collecting supplies as well as for evacuating the wounded.

A valuable unit, it was chosen from among the divisions to lead the breakthrough for *Cobra.* The *USAAF's* preliminary *carpet bombing* attacked their lines dramatically on July 24 and then 25, putting 814 of his men out of action, including 164 men suffering from battle fatigue. Nevertheless, it managed to seize Hébécrevon before progressing southwards. The opposition remained vigorous, since it met a new elite group, namely the *2.Panzerdivision*, which tried to restore the situation. On July 31, the *743rd Tank Battalion,* the regiment of tanks attached to the *30th US ID,* had only thirteen *Shermans* left, out of the fifty-two of its theoretical supply.

Infantrymen of the 30th US ID were far from powerless against the Panzer or in reducing the enemy's strength. The division actually combined the Sherman 743rd Tank Battalion and the M10 of the 823rd Tank Destroyer Battalion, making almost 100 armoured vehicles.
Photo T. Le Sant

A hidden marksman with a bazooka opens fire on the opposition's positions. Dug in to the embankments of the hedges and following carefully-studied firing plans, the Germans were tough opponents on a battlefield as favourable to the defence as the bocage.
NARA (© Editions Ouest-France - colorisation Graph&ti)

THE ISOLATED BATTALION OF HILL 317

On 7 August, a regiment of the *30th US ID* was swept away by the *Das Reich* but the *GIs* - the majority of the *2nd Bn 120th IR* and *K* company of the *3rd Bn* - managed to hold Hill 314. The battalion's command post fell into German hands. The direction of the defence of this isolated position therefore devolved on Captain Erichson. From these heights dominating Mortain and the surrounding area, the observers in the isolated artillery battalion enabled the Americans to cause chaos on the enemy channels of communication. The Hill 317 defenders had their ammunition and food supplies replenished by air, although half of the drops were carried out in areas controlled by the Germans. Using an ingenious method, the artillery sent medical equipment to the besieged *GIs* using shells normally used for leaflets. Erichson's men were also supplied by the Norman civilians who had also been caught in the trap. They did not give in, and rejected the *SS's* request to surrender on the afternoon of August 9. Relieved on August 12, the battalion had suffered the loss of three hundred of its seven hundred men.

The division then took up position around Mortain, right on the axis of the German *Lüttich*counter-offensive, triggered on August 7. It gave proof of its value in the course of these battles. The infantrymen of the *30th US ID*, working with the artillery and the air force, managed to stop a powerful and determined *Panzer* counter-offensive. Taking into account the available American reserves and the power of the *US Army*, as well as the Allied air supremacy, it was doomed to failure, no matter what.

After this setback, the *30th US ID* headed east, via Mortagne, Dreux and Évreux. During the pursuit towards the *Reich*, it reached Liege (in Belgium), on September10, then Maastricht, in the Netherlands, two days later. In October, it took part in the battle of Aix-la-Chapelle then, from December onwards, was engaged in the Battle of the Bulge. Crossing the Rhine on March 24 1945, its participation in the German campaign ended on the Elbe, where it met up with the Soviet forces. At the end of the war, this unit was regarded as the best *Infantry Division* having fought in Europe.

4th Canadian Armoured Division

Offshoot of the *4th Canadian Infantry Division*, the *4th Canadian Armoured Division* was raised in 1942. It was then placed under the command of Major-General Worthington. It is initially intended to supply it with Canadian-designed *Ram* tanks, prior to equipping the division with *Shermans*, the standard tank of all nationalities in the Allied armoured divisions. The day before the Landings, its training had been so long delayed that the Canadian commanders believed that it was not sufficiently operational to be engaged in the first weeks of the battle. Placed under the command of Major-General Kitching, it did not land until the end of July. The division failed in its first attacks in front of La Hogue and Tilly-La-Campagne at the beginning of August.

A moment of relaxation before the assault. The 4th Canadian Armoured Division's baptism of fire was tough. At the beginning of August, it was engaged in the sector of La Hogue and its wood, overlooking the plain of the top of the Bourguébus ridge.
Coll. T. Le Sant

The restrained insignia of the 4th Canadian Armoured Division: a simple green rectangle. Coll. T. Le Sant

The 4th Canadian Division participated actively in the closing of the Falaise pocket. German prisoners captured at the Quantité crossroads at Saint-Lambert-sur-Dive, situated on one of the main routes for the retreat of the 7.Army out of the 'Kessel' have put their hands on their heads, probably at the request of the photographer. Still wearing their helmets and all their equipment, they have clearly only just laid down their arms. PAC

It took part in *Operations Totalize* and *Tractable* which, from August 7 to 17, finally allowed the Allies to repel the German presence and to take Falaise. *Operation Totalize* represented the unit's first major commitment, and the results obtained were disappointing, particularly because the losses are very heavy. The operation was marked by a tragic misunderstanding, since the rear echelons of the division were accidentally bombed by the *USAAF*.

During *Operation Tractable*, in the course of which it was again struck by friendly fire, it crossed the Laizon and broke through the enemy front, albeit at the cost of heavy losses. It captured approximately one thousand Germans. Leaving Falaise in the hands of the *2nd Can. Div.*, the *4th Can. Arm. Div* headed eastwards, together with the Poles. On the 18th, it seized Trun.

OPERATION *TOTALIZE*: CARNAGE ON HILL 140

The offensive began in the night of August 7 to 8. Armoured columns - with infantrymen perched on the *Kangaroo* armoured cars for the first time - were initially delayed by traffic bottlenecks. A few tanks were lost at Cintheaux, taken by the *29th Canadian Armoured Reconnaissance Regiment,* in a battle during which the *Panzer* ace, Michael Wittmann, was killed. The breakthrough was not achieved; on the following day, August 8, the effort was continued. A tragedy then befell Worthington's force, which was a battalion of infantry and an armoured battalion, the *British Colombia.* Its objective was Hill 195, a strategic position which had to be taken to secure the advance on Falaise. The column lost its way, and a tragic misunderstanding occurred: it moved into position on Hill 140, believing it to be Hill 195. Worthington's force, encircled, was subjected to violent counter-attacks, while the relief sent by the *1st Polish Armoured Division* was repulsed. Forty-seven *Shermans* were destroyed at the end of the *British Colombia's* first fight.

A Sherman tank of the South Alberta Regiment passes the smoking wreck of a less lucky Sherman. The photograph was taken at Saint-Lambert-sur-Dive, where Currie arrived with a small troop of fifteen Shermans and 125 men. PAC

The South Alberta Regiment was one of the units of the 4th Canadian Armoured Division.
Coll. T. Le Sant

Major Currie then directed a column of 175 men towards Saint-Lambert-sur-Dive where, cut off, he pushed back the attacks of an opponent in dire straits, who was attempting to flee the cauldron of Falaise. The first arrivals were the abandoned *Shermans.* Separated from the infantry, these Canadian tanks had been circling one another to cover themselves from the German infantrymen who were attacking them. It took the intervention of the artillery, which fired on its own tanks, to get rid of their attackers. In the course of the operation, Currie captured two thousand prisoners. Apart from that, there were three hundred German dead and about fifty enemy vehicles destroyed, including seven *Panzers* and twelve 88mm guns. This feat of arms meant that he was awarded a *Victoria Cross.* Another column progressed toward the Poles, cut off on Mont Ormel. The failure of this operation caused Kitching to be sacked. He was replaced by Major-General Foster. The evacuation movement was completed during the afternoon of August 21 when the Canadians joined the Poles, impenetrably and definitively closing the Falaise pocket.

Corporal McAllister, who single-handedly captured 160 Germans, managed to lay his hands on a Luger, a highly coveted weapon. He is sitting on a gun, probably satisfied with what he had done. Victory came at a price for the Canadians, who suffered very badly between Caen and Saint-Lambert in that terrible month of August 1944. PAC

On August 27, the division crossed the Seine at Elbeuf before turning north. It then took part in the fighting for the Breskens Pocket, on the Scheldt estuary, and then in the Netherlands . In April 1945, it was the campaign in the heart of the *Reich*. The *4th Armoured Division* was in the vicinity of Oldenburg, in northern Germany, when the cease-fire was declared.

A Canadian-built Chevrolet C8A 4 x 4 lorry with its two-tone camouflage. It was an HUP (Heavy Utility Personnel) transporter. Coll. T. Le Sant

53rd British Infantry Divison

The insignia of the 53rd Welsh Division represents the three brigades of the division (triangle and bars shooting up) as well as the horizontal bar at the base.
Coll. T. Le Sant

This soldier of the 53rd Welsh Division is armed with the famous Sten sub-machine gun. The division had to fight hard in the Odon and Orne sectors.

This territorial division, recruited in Wales, was raised in 1939. It undertook coastal defence missions from 1939 to 1943, first in Northern Ireland and then in the south of England. The months preceding the Landings were devoted to manoeuvres and training for the invasion. The storm of June 19 delayed its crossing, however.

On June 28, Major-General Ross's *53rd Welsh* was ready for action. It went into action the next day, in the bridgehead established on the Odon by the *15th Scottish*. On July 8, the Welsh, supported by the *34th Tank Brigade's Churchills*, had to seize Évrecy in the context of *Operation Greenline*. They faced fierce resistance from German infantry formations. Nine days later, they were pushed back with losses, during an unsuccessful attempt. However, *Operation Greenline* forced first Rommel, then Kluge to retain the *II.SS Panzerkorps* in the Odon sector, while *Operation Goodwood* was launched on the right bank of the Orne.

This Bren Carrier, followed by a column of prisoners, including Fallschirmjäger, symbolises the victory brought off by the Allies at Falaise. For the civilians, free at last, the roads were about to fill up with the comings and goings of Allied units, among which there was a formidable amount of motorisation. IWM

Soldiers of the 53rd Welsh Division. The infantry divisions are often largely forgotten in the battle of Normandy. They nevertheless supplied the big battalions of the armies which faced each other for months. Ten of the seventeen Anglo-Canadian divisions were infantry divisions. Coll. T. Le Sant

AUGUST 3: A HELPING HAND AT BON-REPOS

Apart from the major offensives, the infantry units' daily round consisted of raids and sporadic fighting. Preceding the thrust which took them towards the Falaise pocket, a raid carried out by a company of the *4th Welsh* was typical. The support was considerable: four artillery regiments, machine guns and mortars, a tank squadron and two troops of *Churchill Crocodiles* with their terrifying flamethrowers. The mission, launched toward Bon-Repos, consisted of the capture of a minimum of fifteen prisoners, so as to establish whether or not the *10.SS Panzer-Regiment* was still on the front line. The raid was carried out according to plan. If no Germans were found in the village, the opposing positions were to be removed, although cooperation between the armoured cars and the infantry was compromised by a delay in getting the *Churchills* into position. Seventeen prisoners were brought back. Some thirty Germans were killed. The British lost four tanks and thirty-two men (one of whom was killed). So far as this was concerned, Lieutenant-Colonel Williams, commander of the *4th Welsh,* did not observe anything out of the ordinary. There was no particular incident to mention. As for the Germans, there was nothing new in their defensive tactics. The battle of Normandy was made up in this way of many local battles, often carried out by infantry divisions, the great forgotten force of the battle.

The *53rd Welsh Division* remained in the Odon salient for the rest of July. The fighting was unusually violent. At Bon-Repos, a German assault almost completely wiped out a company of the *1/5 Welsh.* On July 23, the Welsh carried out a raid as far as this same Bon-Repos crossroads, forcing the Germans to retreat to Esquay-Notre-Dame.

In August, they took part in the thrust which drove the enemy into the Falaise pocket. They took Hill 112, abandoned by the Germans, and crossed the Orne at Grimbosq. One single *Tiger* and a handful of infantry from the *271.ID* held them at bay at Bois-Halbout for a whole day. However, their remarkable progress created a six-kilometre salient as far as Nécy. It was on August 16 that Captain Watkins, the only surviving officer of his company, arrived, sten-gun in hand, to neutralize a canon anti-tank gun after having led his men past a mine field. Repulsing a bayonet counter-attack, he rejoined the Allied lines. This feat led to his award of the prestigious *Victoria Cross.*

The Seine was crossed on August 30 at Muids. The Netherlands campaign was particularly arduous and hard-fought. It took the division four days of intense fighting to seize the town of 's-Hertogenbosch in October 1944. Sent in support of American units during the German counter-offensive in the Ardennes, the *53rd British ID* took part in the battle for Germany. It was in Hamburg at the time of the surrender. Its losses, since the Battle of Normandy, had risen to 9,849 men. The British nicknamed these Welsh *'Monty's Darlings'* because they performed every task assigned to them. Evocatively, on their side the Germans called them *"Monty's Butchers"*.

The Carden-Loyd Universal Carrier, or Bren Carrier, was a highly versatile machine, found in all the British formations. Each infantry battalion had thirty-three. The device, of which 70,000 were manufactured, could reach 51 km/h. Photo T. Le Sant

9.Panzerdivision

The *9.Panzer* took part in the Western Campaign in 1940, first in the Netherlands and then in France. It was then engaged in the Balkans, in April 1941, before preparing to fight against the Red Army. It took part in major operations in the Soviet Union, until January 1944. Survivor of the Hell of the Eastern Front, the *9.Panzer* was reconstituted, from April 1944, in the Carcassonne region. On June 6, its strength was still only 12,768 men and 123 *Panzers* and *Sturmgeschützen.* The division, which was not yet operational, was kept in reserve in the south of France with the *11.Panzerdivision.* The unit was, however, gradually strengthened. It was supplied with 161 *Panzer IV* and *Panthers* in Normandy, as well as 5 *Sturmgeschützen* and 9 *Mardern.* The reconnaissance unit, a formation which was very often strong within the *Panzerdivisionen,* was particularly well equipped since it included 15 armored personnel carriers, nearly 70 half-tracks and, above all, 28 *Luchs,* a latest-generation reconnaissance tank, as rare as the *Puma* which were supplied to the reconnaissance battalions of the *Panzer Lehr* and the *2.Panzer.* At the end, in late July 1944, with the *9.Panzer,* the German army still had a powerful unit which had not yet been called to the Front of the invasion.

On July 27, the development of *Operation Cobra* forced the German high command to send this division to Normandy. The *Panthers,* who were then en route to the south of France, had to be loaded back on to trains and sent independently toward the Front.

On June 6, the 9. Panzer-Division was billeted in the Avignon.sector. Members of a tank crew as experienced as this were trained to fight against the Anglo-Americans. However, the war in Normandy was nothing like their experiences on the Eastern Front.
Coll. T. Le Sant

Waiting in ambush, this Panzer was almost impossible to detect before it opened fire. The 9. Panzer had to be split up and rushed in, in an attempt to oppose the tide of Patton's 3rd US Army, which threatened first Le Mans then Alencon. Coll. P. Tiquet

In fact, this powerful battalion was never engaged within its division, and its strike force was wasted and scattered. On August 14, when it had not yet taken part in any engagement, the *Panther* battalion had only 25 operational machines (out of 79) and was attached to the *116.Panzer*. The bulk of Generalleutnant Jolasse's *9.Panzer* therefore left Avignon to make for the Front by rail, but its journey was thwarted by the omnipresent Allied air force as well as by acts of sabotage carried out by the *FFI*.

The unit was scattered in Normandy, and fighting against Patton's *3rd Army* between Le Mans and Alencon soon weakened it. On August 6, its units were spread out over 50 kilometres between Domfront and Montsûrs. The strength of the *Wehrmacht* was very strained in that sector, and Jolasse was left virtually alone with the weak *708.ID*. Under those conditions, the *9.Panzer* under the command of Oberst Sperling, could do nothing to stop the American breakthrough.

Because of this, the clashes against Leclerc's 2nd *DB* were particularly costly for the Germans, as well as for the Allies, who lost almost forty tanks on August 11. From August 16 onwards, the order was received to fall back and to take position to the south-west of Paris. The division came away from the battle of Normandy very weakened, with barely a dozen tanks escaping from the trap of the Falaise pocket. In addition, contrary to the other *Panzer* divisions, its support and logistics units were wiped out, causing a considerable setback for the maintenance of the operational unit. The *9.Panzer* had lost between 3,500 and 4,000 men, out of 14,500.

This photograph, taken in Russia, shows that the 9. Panzer-Division , an elite unit, had had to be re-equipped. If many Panzers were lacking in June 1944, the formation which advanced to the front in July 1944 was very well supplied with tanks. DR

The war was not over yet for this division, which had been in all of the campaigns. It confronted the Americans in the Aix-la-Chapelle area in the autumn, and then played its part in the second wave during the Battle of the Bulge. In March 1945, it vainly opposed the American bridgehead established at Remagen. The *9.Panzer* was lost with the *Heeres-Gruppe B* in the Ruhr pocket.

Number of operational *Panzer* and *Panzerjäger*

August 9	about 50
August 21	12

FIGHTING IN THE FOREST OF ÉCOUVES

The *9.Panzer* tried in vain to oppose the taking of Alençon. The French of Leclerc's division seized it in the morning of August 12. The *Panzer* division was hiding in the forest of Écouves, a fairly large forest on a terrain which was favourable to the defence. The Germans were attacked from several directions. While one column attacked from the south, another French unit skirted the forest, entered it at Sées and then took the German defence from the rear, in the forest. The fighting was fierce, particularly at la Croix de Médavy, and continued until August 13. *Panzers, Paks* and *Panzerfaüsten* cost French losses, but their fight was in vain. The *9.Panzer's* strike force, already considerably weakened, was virtually destroyed in the course of those combats.

2e Division blindée française

An officer of the 2nd DB. The uniform and equipment are American. Only his red MP cap distinguishes him from his American comrades.
Coll. T. Le Sant

This other officer from Leclerc's division Leclerc is wearing a headgear which betrays his nationality: a kepi, typically French.
Coll. T. Le Sant

The *2nd Armoured Division* was officially raised on August 24 1943 from a core of Free French units which had fought in Africa under Leclerc. Twelve thousand men of the African Army, whose wait-and-see policy had disgusted Leclerc, joined his French Foreign Legion unit. The black troops were replaced by AFN conscripts, and those who had escaped from France arrived via Spain. Three thousand six hundred and four men, a quarter of the unit, were Moroccans or Algerians. The *13th Medical Battalion*, the *'Rochambelles'*, were unusual in that they were exclusively female recruits. Leclerc organized his division into tactical groupings similar to the American *Combat Commands* : Lieutenant-Colonel Dio's *GTD*; Colonel de Langlade's *GTL*; Colonel Billotte's *GTV*; and Rémy's *GTR*. Landing on *Utah* early in August, the *2nd DB* began to move towards Le Mans. Its first contact with the enemy was serious: bombed by the *Luftwaffe* while it was still bivouacked, the *GTD* lost 129 men, of whom five were killed.

The *2nd DB* was involved in the encircling manoeuvre to trap the German forces in the Falaise pocket. The Allied attack was irresistible, and Leclerc liberated Alençon on August 12 at the same time as the *5th US Arm. Div.* took Sées. Argentan also seemed to be on the verge of falling, but the *GTV* took a road allocated to the *5th US Arm. Div.*, which then lost six precious hours - which the Germans used to fortify Argentan. The French vanguard, which had entered the town, giving the inhabitants premature joy, was thrown back out again, so the chance to tighten the net more quickly was lost. Bradley ordered a halt to progress, to Patton's annoyance.

Leclerc landing on Utah Beach. He was welcomed by General Walker. In the second row can be seen a French officer, who is wearing the motorised troops' helmet as worn in 1940. The fighting led by Leclerc was that of an army with its pride restored. NARA

Many victories were taken by the *2nd DB*. The *9.Panzer*, already badly mauled to the south of Alençon, was wiped out in the forest of Écouves. At Carrouges, the *GTD* surprised a column of the *Das Reich*. Near Montmerrei, the *GTD* destroyed a dozen *Panzer IVs*. The French only suffered very light losses.

THE TAKING OF ALENÇON

On the evening of the 11th, the *2nd DB* was on the edge of the forest of Perseigne. Leclerc, collecting as much information as possible from the local people on the possible routes and strength of the enemy, meticulously prepared the next day's attack, which was to enable him to take Alençon. At 04:30, the vanguard, guided by a young civilian, was sent on Alençon. The bridges on the Sarthe were quickly taken and a German column was surprised by the French advance. Colonel Dio's battle group was responsible for cleaning the pockets of resistance before relief was provided by the *90th US ID*. The fall of the town, which had been the logistics base of the *VII. Army*, was a disaster for the *Wehrmacht* in Normandy. In addition, the threat posed by the *15th US Corps* to the rear of the German forces in Normandy became clearer.

This Sherman M4 (105 mm) sets its tracks on the sand of Normandy after being hoisted out of the hold of the LST which had brought it across the English Channel. The hour of revenge on the Germans had finally come! NARA

This fine line-up of armoured cars of the 2nd DB illustrates the impotence of the Luftwaffe, who would never have let such a great opportunity pass in 1940. Leclerc's drive towards Alençon, then Argentan, caused very heavy losses among the Germans. Archives du Calvados

The order was finally received for the *15th US Corps* to march on Falaise. On August 19, the *GTL* was engaged towards Exmes-Omméel, not far from Mont Ormel where the Poles, who had closed the trap on the *VII. Army*, were fighting. The French artillery struck the retreating German columns, who were trying to escape from the cauldron of Falaise. The baptism of fire of the*2nd DB* was therefore a success. The Battle of Normandy cost Leclerc 866 men, of whom 135 were killed, as well as the loss of 76 tanks and armoured vehicles, 27 half-tracks, 7 guns and 133 vehicles. According to its somewhat excessive claims, losses inflicted on the enemy were 4,500 killed and 8,800 taken prisoner, with 117 tanks, 79 guns and 750 vehicles destroyed or captured.

Leclerc's spirit, however, was no longer in Normandy. From August 19, in fact, the Resistance had started uprisings in Paris. De Gaulle, anxious to establish his legitimacy, wanted a trustworthy unit, commanded by a Gaullist right from the start, to control the situation in the capital. Before even obtaining authorisation of his American superiors, Leclerc sent the Guillebon detachment of 250 men to Rambouillet. On August 22, Bradley authorised Leclerc to charge on Paris. He therefore sent the agreed message: 'Gilbrius'. The first units of the *2nd DB* entered the capital during the evening of August 24. The following day, Paris was liberated.

The war continued for the *2nd DB.* There were victorious battles in Lorraine, at Dompaire, then the liberation of Strasbourg. After a posting on the Atlantic, the *2nd DB* charged to the heart of the *Reich* and penetrated the *Führer's* hideaway in Berchtesgaden.

The insignia of the French 2nd Armoured Division: a cross of Lorraine, the symbol of the Free French, on the background of a map of France. Coll. T. Le Sant

The Sherman 'Valois' of the 2nd. DB is now a monument at the Croix-de-Médavy crossroads in the Ecouves forest, where it was put out of action on August 13, 1944. Photo T. Le Sant

1st Polish Armoured Division

The uniform of this tank officer of the 1st Polish Armoured Division is completely consistent with that of a British unit. Only the insignia and badges of rank are different. The British army armed and equipped the new Polish army, which fought in Normandy and in Italy. Coll. T. Le Sant

Major-General Maczek's *1st Polish Armoured Division* was raised in Scotland in1942 from survivors of the 1939 - 40 debacles in Poland and France, former prisoners from Soviet camps, escapees from Nazi camps, and volunteers.

The division's 16,000 men, 381 tanks and 4,431 vehicles landed on August 2, at Arromanches and Courseulles. The Poles, highly motivated, were keen to cross swords with the Germans. Their baptism of fire took place on August 8, in the second phase of *Operation Totalize*. The Polish attack was aimed at a series of villages to the south of the Bourguébus ridge. That day, the *SS* taught the newly-engaged

The insignia of the 1st Polish Armoured Division. Coll. T. Le Sant

With its powerful 17-pounder, the Sherman Firefly could overcome any Panzer. Nevertheless, sixty tanks were lost during the first two days of the division's engagement.
Coll. T. Le Sant

division a sharp lesson. Forty tanks were hit, and the division was stopped at Saint-Aignan-de-Crasmesnil. The following day, it had to face the infiltration of enemy infantry, and another twenty armoured vehicles were lost. The losses were, however, limited to thirteen more tanks during the counter-attacks from August 11 to 13. The Poles were then engaged on the right flank of the main attack of *Tractable* . They managed to move forward quickly, crossing the Dives at Jort. On the 17th, they were located at Norrey-en-Auge.

A Polish tank crewman's helmet emblazoned with the insignia of the Polish forces in exile, worn on combatants' helmets in Normandy as well as Italy (where an army corps fought at Monte Cassino).
Private collection.

Maczek received the order to seize Trun, an essential crossroads for the retreating Germans. On the 18th, he had to ensure that Chambois was captured, to deprive the enemy of the last way out of the Falaise pocket. The division's flanks were unsecured, since the Canadians were still several kilometres in the rear. Chambois was reached, then conquered, after a hard struggle on August 19. During the evening, a connection was established with the *GIs* of the *90th US ID*. Virtually cut off from their own side, the Polish handed 1,300 prisoners over to the Americans and occupied Hill 113. Another battle group reached Mont Ormel, at the mouth of the *VII Army's* evacuation corridor . The Poles were able to hold their positions, despite the Germans' furious attacks. Thanks to the efforts of the *2.* and *9.SS Panzerdivisionen*, one column was able to break through in the Mont Ormel sector, and another at Chambois; however they did not succeed in taking those positions. Many German soldiers were forced to escape on foot, in small groups. On August 22, it was all over: the German defeat was complete. German losses reached 1,800 men in the Hill 113 sector, where the Poles captured General Elfeldt, commander of the *LXXXIV. Korps*.

MONT ORMEL

On reaching the peak of Mont Ormel, the Poles surprised and wiped out a German convoy of over two kilometres. No fewer than 87 armoured personnel carriers and 1,500 men, under the command of Lieutenant-Colonel Stefanowicz, were entrenched on this knoll. The Germans fought against the Polish positions on Hill 262 and Boijos for three days, attacking from both the inside and the outside of the pocket. If the *II. Fallschirm-Korps* managed to extricate itself from the trap, after bloody hand-to-hand night combat, it was at the cost of a large part of its heavy equipment. The Poles effected a real massacre in their assailants' ranks but, chivalrously, they allowed a convoy evacuating their wounded enemies to pass. However, while Warsaw, rebelling as the Red Army approached, was reduced to rubble by the Nazis, it seems that the Poles did not hesitate to kill any German prisoners whose military record betrayed their participation in the invasion of Poland in 1939. When the Canadian relief finally arrived, there were only 114 able-bodied men left and about thirty operational tanks among the defenders. Maczek had lost 352 men killed, 114 missing and 1,002 injured. From then on, Mont Ormel was known as *Maczuga'*, the Polish for 'club'.

Chambois: contact was established between the Poles and the Americans. On the left, Lieutenant Wladyslaw Klaptocz of the 10th Polish Dragoons and, on the right, Major Leonard C. Dull, of the 2nd Bn, 359th IR of the 90th US ID. The Falaise pocket was finally closed! NARA

The shoulder title indicating nationality, worn on the battle-dress. Coll. T. Le Sant

By successfully hampering the German retreat, the role of the *1st Polish Armoured Division* was indubitably decisive in the final phase of the battle of Normandy. One might reasonably ask if Monty, to save British lives, did not deliberately choose to entrust this suicidal mission to the Poles. After a few days of well-deserved rest, the Seine was crossed on August 31. The division continued its campaign in Belgium and Holland. In April 1945, it entered Germany in the Emsland sector. On May 6 1945, it obtained the surrender of the important naval base at Wilhelmshaven. At the end of hostilities, most of the soldiers in the division opted to remain in the West, rather than returning to a Poland which had passed into Soviet control.

L'US Cavalry en Normandie

The first American tank to be provided with a hedge-cutter device was an M5 Stuart, similar to the one shown below. The invention of this decisive innovation is generally attributed to Sergeant Culin, of the United States Cavalry ... NARA

In addition to the divisional reconnaissance formations, several units of the American cavalry were operational in Normandy. These units, the *Cavalry Groups*, were eight in number: the *2nd, 3rd, 4th, 6th, 15th, 102nd, 106th and 113th Cavalry Groups*. The organisation was the same for all: two battalions with several light vehicles, being mainly M8 Light Armoured Cars, jeeps and half-tracks. In theory, each corps had its own integral *Cavalry Group*.

The purpose of these reconnaissance formations was to secure long-distance information, to supply advice on the opposition's dispositions, and to carry out protective missions on the army corps' or the division's flanks. If the missions entrusted to the *Cavalry Groups* were initially limited by the difficulties of the *bocage*, the *Cobra* breakthrough allowed them to give free rein to their vocation, often with a certain amount of audacity.

THE FLANK-GUARD OF THE BREAKTHROUGH

From July 30 to August 4, the *113th Cavalry Group,* under the command of the *28th US ID,* secured communications with the neighbouring units. The *113th Cavalry Reconnaissance Squadron*, for its part, operated in conjunction with the *2nd US Arm. Div.,* carrying out genuine reconnaissance missions to the west of the Vire, despite the increase of traps and mines on the roads. On August 13, the whole *113th Cavalry Group* headed for Mortain, then established a mobile screen for the benefit of the *30th US ID* - particularly between the latter's regiments - up to Domfront, taken by the cavalry after hard fighting. On August 19, the *113th* once again had to precede the *30th US ID* as far as Brézolles, where soldiers from the infantry division had to be taken in lorries. By this encircling movement, the *19th US Corps* sought to cut off the retreat of the German forces. This 150-mile run was carried out in the evening: contact was made with the enemy and a series of roadblocks was set up to ensure good progress in the deployment of the *30th US ID's* infantry. The following day, August 20, the *113th Cavalry Group* was scattered over some fifty kilometres to provide a solution of continuous communications between the *19th* and *5th US Corps* from Verneuil to Sées. The unit was then directed north, in the direction of the British forces, to secure the cleaning of the crossing area, including the Breteuil and Conches forests.

The first American cavalry unit to take part in the battle of Normandy was Colonel Tully's *4th Cavalry Group*, which was actually the first *US Army* unit to disembark on June 6 1944. Attached to the *7th US Corps*, the cavalry came ashore on the Îles Saint-Marcouf at 04:00. The fear that the German defences would endanger the assault on *Utah Beach* proved unfounded: the islands were undefended, and the only losses were due to mines. Part of the unit landed on the continent, with the mission of establishing communications with the airborne forces dropped during the night and providing liaison between the *82nd* and *101st US Airborne Divisions*. The *4th Cavalry* was involved in support of the *4th* and *9th US ID* during the fighting for Cherbourg. It was operating with the *2nd US Armored Division* during the breakthrough of *Operation Cobra*, ensuring the security of this unit's flank during its charge within the German lines. The *4th* fulfilled similar tasks with the *1st US ID*, also making good use of its reconnaissance toward Mortain.

Colonel Dolph's *102nd Cavalry Group* fought within the *5th US Corps*. It landed on *Omaha Beach* on June 8. Its first mission was reconnaissance beyond the bridgehead for the benefit of the *1st US ID*. The *102nd Cavalry Group* protected the corps' flank during the general advance on the Front at the end of July 1944. The *106th Cavalry Group, 'Patton's Bastards'*, commanded by Colonel Wilson, was attached to the *8th US Corps*. It engaged in battle for the first time on July 2. After having contributed to cleaning out the pockets of resistance following the breakthrough of *Operation Cobra*, the *106th* passed by Avranches and headed for Rennes. Its mission is to bridge the gap which had formed between the *8th US Corps* and the *15th US Corps*. Transferred to this latter corps, the *106th* was the first American unit to enter Le Mans, on August 6. While the army corps returned to the north, to shut the *VII. Army* in a trap, the *106th* acted as flank guards. Colonel Reybold's *15th Cavalry Group*, in its turn, landed

An M8 armoured car from a cavalry unit passes through a ruined village. Advancing audaciously in flank-guard, or at the head of the American forces, troops of the US Cavalry showed their under-estimated courage. Coll. T. Le Sant

on *Utah Beach* on July 5 1944 and ran patrols at the rear of the *1st US Army*, before taking part in the dash of *Cobra*, operating in Brittany and then on the Loire. Colonel Fickett's *6th Cavalry Group*, attached to the *15th US Corps* in Normandy, held an essential role for Patton: that of *Army Information Service* - because the unit's patrols informed the leader of the *3rd US Army* by radio of operations, and of the location of its most advanced formations. In the end, they were known as *'Patton's Household Cavalry'.* Colonel Biddle's *113th Cavalry Group* was attached to the *19th US Corps.* They were particularly involved in the difficult fighting

The M8 armoured car with its 20 mm gun and its .50 calibre machine gun (12.7 mm) formed the backbone of the US Cavalry units. Photo T. Le Sant

An American cavalry unit's half-track crossing a Norman village to the cheers of French civilians: a scene which was endlessly repeated during the month of August 1944.
Coll. T. Le Sant

between Vire and la Taute, then towards Saint-Lô, in July 1944, before contributing to the surrounding of the German forces engaged in Normandy; not without having had to face serious fighting, such as in Villebaudon. Colonel Reed's *2nd Cavalry Group* - *'Patton's Ghosts'* -was engaged from July onwards, as was Colonel Polk's *3rd Cavalry Group*, the *'Brave Rifles'* after *Cobra*.

The *Cavalry Groups* were then involved in all the campaigns: in Lorraine, at Aix-la-Chapelle, in Alsace, in the Ardennes and then in the heart of the *Reich*. The *106th* finished the war in Austria, where the unit freed the king of Belgium, Leopold III, from captivity. On April 30 1945, the *113th* established communications with the Soviets on the Elbe, making the first contact between the *9th US Army* and the Red Army.

LIST OF DIVISIONS

BRITISH DIVISIONS

6th Airborne Division : Gale
3rd ID : Rennie (13 juin : Cass ; 23 juin : Whistler)
50th Northumbrian ID : Graham
51th Highland ID : Bullen-Smith
43rd Wessex ID : Thomas
15th Scottich ID : Mac Millan
49th West Riding ID : Barker
53rd Welsh ID : Ross
59th Staffordshire ID : Lyne
3rd Canadian ID : Keller
2nd Canadian ID : Foulkes

7th Armoured Div. Desert Rats : Erskine (3 août : Verney)
11th Armoured Div. Taurus Pursant : Roberts
Guards Armoured Div. : Adair
79th Armoured Div. : Hobart
1st Polish Armoured Div. : Maczek
4th Canadian Armoured Div. : Kitching

4th Armoured Br. : Currie (26 juin : Carver)

AMERICAN DIVISIONS

82nd Airborne Division All American : Ridgway
101th Airborne Division Screaming Eagles : Taylor
1st ID Big Red One : Huebner
2nd ID Indian Head : Robertson
4th ID Ivy : Barton
29th ID Blue and Gray : Gerhardt
90th ID Texas-Ocklahoma or Though Men : Landrum
79th ID Lorraine : Wyche
9th ID Varsity : Eddy
83rd ID Ohio : Macon
30th ID Old Hickory : Hobbs
8th ID Golden Arrow : Mac Mahon (mi juillet : Stroh)
28th ID Keystone : Cota
35th ID Santa Fe : Baade
5th ID Red Diamond : Irwin
80th ID Blue Ridge : Mac Bride

2nd Armoured Div. Hell on Wheels : Brooks
3rd Armoured Div. Spearhead : Watson (6 août : Rose)
4th Armoured Div. Breakthrough : Wood
5th Armoured Div. Victory : Oliver
6th Armoured Div. Super Sixth : Grow
7th Armoured Div. Lucky Seventh : Mc. D Sylvester
2e DB : Leclerc

GERMAN DIVISIONS

352 ID : Kraiss
716 ID : Richter
711 ID : Reichert
243 ID : Hellmich
(2 juillet : Klosterkemper)
77 ID : Stegmann
(2 juillet : Bacherer)
91 LD : Koenig

272 ID : Schaft
709 ID : von Schlieben

275 ID : Schmidt
265 ID : Düvert
266 ID : Spang
343 (élts) : Rauch
708 ID : Wilk
276 ID : Badinski
346 ID : Diestel

353 ID : Mahlmann
85 ID : Chill
89 ID : Heinrichs

84 ID : Menny

271 ID : Danhauser
277 ID : Praum
(août : Viebig)
363 ID : Dettling
326 ID : von Drabisch-Waetcher
331 ID : Steinmüller
16 LFD : Sievers
17 LFD : Hoecker
3 FJD : Schimpf
5 FJD : Wilke
6 FJD : Heyking

21 PZD : Feuchtinger
PZ Lehr : Bayerlein
2 PZD : von Lüttwitz
116 PZD : von Schwerin
9 PZD : Jolasse
1 SS PZD Leibstandarte Adolf Hitler : Wisch
2 SS PZD Das Reich : Lammerding
9 SS PZD Hohenstaufen : Bittrich (28 juin : Müller)
10 SS PZD Frunsberg : Harmel
12 SS PZD Hitlerjugend : Witt (14 juin : Meyer)
17 SS PZGD Götz von Berlichingen : Ostendorff (19 juin : Baum)

SELECTIVE BIBLIOGRAPHY

BOOKS

BEEVOR Antony, *D-Day et la bataille de Normandie*, Calmann-Lévy, 2009.
BENAMOU Jean-Pierre, *Album Mémorial : Bataille de Caen*, Heimdal, 1988.
BERNAGE Georges et CADEL Georges, *Cobra, la bataille décisive, Normandie 1944*, Heimdal, 1984.
BERNAGE Georges et FRANCOIS Dominique, *Utah Beach, Sainte-Mère-Église*, Heimdal, 2004.
BERNAGE Georges, *Objectif Carentan*, Heimdal, 2010.
BERNAGE Georges, *Goodwood, Bombardement géant brise-Panzers*, Heimdal, 1994.
BERNAGE Georges *et alii*, *Objectif Sainte-Mère-Église*, Heimdal, 1993.
BERNAGE Georges *et alli*, *Le Couloir de la mort, Falaise – Argentan 1944*, Heimdal, 2007.
BERNAGE Georges *et alii*, *Album Mémorial : Overlord, Jour J en Normandie*, Heimdal, 1993.
BERNAGE Georges *et alii*, *Album Mémorial : Bataille de Normandie*, Heimdal, 1994.
BOUCHERY Jean *et alii*, *Les Paras du D-Day. Britanniques, Canadiens, Français*, Histoire & Collections, 2004.
BOUCHERY Jean, *Le Tommy de la Libération*, Histoire & Collections, 2013.
BRANDO Mark, *Vanguard of the Crusade. The 101st Airborne Division in World War II*, Heimdal, 2012.
CARRUTHERS Bob, *The German Army in Normandy*, Coda Books Ltd, 2012.
COPP Terry, *Fields of Fire, The Canadians in Normandy*, University of Toronto Press, 2003.
D'ESTE Carlo, *Histoire du Débarquement*, Perrin, 2013.
DAGLISH Ian, *Operation Bluecoat*, Leo Cooper, 2003.
DAGLISH Ian, *Operation Epsom*, Pen & Sword, 2007.
DAGLISH Ian, *Operation Goodwood*, Pen & Sword, 2005.
DESCHODT Christophe *et alii*, *Les Paras du D-Day. Les Américains*, Histoire & Collections, 2010.
DE TREZ Michel, *At the Point of No Return. Pictorial History of the American Paratroopers in the Invasion of Normandy*, D-Day Publishing, 1994.
EISENHOWER Dwight D., *Croisade en Europe*, traduit de l'anglais par Paule de Beaumont, Paris, Robert Laffont, 1949.
FORTIN Ludovic, *Les Chars britanniques en Normandie*, Histoire & Collections, 2005.
FORTIN Ludovic, *Opérations Totalize et Tractable*, Histoire & Collections, 2008.
FOWLER Will, *Pegasus Bridge*, Raid n° 11, Osprey Publishing, 2010.
FÜRBRINGER Herbert, *9.SS Panzerdivision*, Heimdal, 1984.
GAWNE Jonathan, *Jour J à l'aube. Les Troupes d'assaut américaines en Normandie*, Histoire & Collections, 1998.
GRIESSER Volker, *Les Lions de Carentan*, Heimdal, 2006.
GUARD Julie (sous la direction de), *Airborne, World War II, Paratroopers in Combat*, Osprey Publishing, 2007.
HART Russell A., *Clash of Arms, How the Allies won in Normandy*, University of Oklahoma Press, 2004.
HART Stephen, *Colossal Cracks, Montgomery's 21st Army Group in Northwest Europe, 1944-45*, Stackpole Books, 2007.
LEFEBVRE Éric, *Les Panzers, Normandie 1944*, Heimdal, 1978.
LELEU Jean-Luc, *10.SS Panzerdivision*, Heimdal, 1999.
LELEU Jean-Luc, *Falaise 16/17 août 1944 : un mythe revisité*, Ysec Éditions, 2007.
LODIEU Didier, *Opération Goodwood*, Histoire & Collections, 2008.
LODIEU Didier, *Mourir pour Saint-Lô*, Histoire & Collections, 2007.
LODIEU Didier, *Objectif : Chambois !*, Ysec Éditions, 2003.
LODIEU Didier, *D'Argentan à la Seine, le bataillon de Panther de la 9.Pz. Div. face au 15e Corps américain*, Ysec Éditions, 2003.
LODIEU Didier, *Combats sur la Seine*, Ysec Éditions, 2007.
LODIEU Didier, *La Massue. Les soldats polonais dans la bataille de Normandie*, Ysec Éditions, 2004.
LODIEU Didier, *L'Odyssée du bataillon de Panther de la 116.Panzerdivision en Normandie, juillet-août 1944*, Histoire & Collections, 2012.
LODIEU Didier, *La 90th US Inf. Div., Tome I, Juin 1944*, Mémorial de Montormel, 2013.
LODIEU Didier, *La 90th US Inf. Div., Tome II, Juillet 1944*, Mémorial de Montormel, 2013.
LUCAS James et BARKER James, *The Battle of Normandy. The Falaise Gap*, Homes and Meir Publishers, 1978.
MAGDELAINE Yann, *Atlas du Débarquement*, Éditions Ouest-France, 2012.
MARIE René, *Villers-Bocage*, Heimdal, 2011.
McMANUS John, *The Americans at Normandy : The Summer of 1944. The American War from the Normandy Beaches to Falaise*, Forge Books, 2013.
MEYER Hubert et BERNAGE Georges, *12.SS Panzerdivision*, Heimdal, 1991.
MILANO Vince et CONNER Bruce, *Normandiefront, D-Day to Saint-Lô through German Eyes*, 2011.
MITCHAM Samuel, *Panzers in Normandy, General Hans Eberbach and the Defense of France, 1944*, Stackpole Books, 2009.
PALLUD Jean-Paul, *Rückmarsch, the German Retreat from Normandy, Then and Now*, After the Battle, 2006.
PERRIGAULT Jean-Claude, *La Panzer Lehr*, Heimdal, 1995.
PIPET Albert, *D'Omaha à Saint-Lô, La Bataille des Haies*, Heimdal, 1980.
PRIME Christophe, *Omaha Beach, 6 juin 1944*, Tallandier, 2011.
QUELLIEN Jean, *Les Américains en Normandie*, OREP Éditions, 2012.
QUETEL Claude (sous la direction de), *Dictionnaire du Débarquement*, Editions Ouest-France, 2011.
RONDEAU Benoît, Invasion !, *Le Débarquement vécu par les Allemands*, Tallandier, 2014
SAUNDERS Hilary St. George, *The Red Beret*, New English Library, 1955 [Michael Joseph Ltd, 1950].
WEIGLEY Russell, *Eisenhower's Lieutenants, The Campaigns of France and Germany, 1944-1945*, Bloomington, Indiana University Press, 1981.
ZALOGA Steven, *Rangers Lead the Way*, Raid n° 1, Osprey Publishing, 2009.
ZETTERLING Niklas, *Normandy 44, German Military Organization, Combat Power and Organizational Effectiveness*, Fedorowicz, 2000.

PERIODICALS

BERNAGE Georges, hors-séries *Historica* nos 68, 69, 70, 71, 74, 75, 106, 111, Heimdal, 2001-2012.
BUFFETAUT Yves, hors-séries *Militaria Magazine* nos 1, 2, 12, 13, 26, 46, 52, 54, 58, 65, 78, Histoire & Collections, 1991-2011.

III. THE BREAKTHROUGH AND THE ALLIED VICTORY

COBRA, THE AMERICAN BREAKTHROUGH

OPERATION *BLUECOAT*

THE MORTAIN COUNTER-ATTACK

LA POUSSÉE SUR FALAISE

THE FALAISE POCKET

THANKS

Thanks to Claude Quétel and Matthieu Biberon, who made this wonderful project possible.
Thanks to Tanguy Le Sant for permission to use photographs from his collection to illustrate this work.
Thanks to Caroline Brou, for her iconographic research work.

Editions OUEST-FRANCE
Lille - Rennes

Éditeur Matthieu Biberon
Coordination éditoriale Caroline Brou
Conception Studio des Éditions Ouest-France
Mise en page Graph&ti, Cesson-Sévigné (35)
Cartographie Patrick Mérienne
Photogravure et colorisations Graph&ti, Cesson-Sévigné (35)
Impression Pollina, Luçon (85)

© 2014, Éditions Ouest-France, Édilarge SA, Rennes
ISBN 978-2-7373-6360-3 • N° d'éditeur 7464.01.4,5.06.14
Dépôt légal : juin 2014
Imprimé en France
www.editionsouestfrance.fr